TOUCHED WITH Fire

An anthology
of poems
compiled by
Jack Hydes

CAMBRIDGE
UNIVERSITY PRESS

To my Mother and Father

CAMBRIDGE
UNIVERSITY PRESS

University Printing House, Cambridge CB2 8BS, United Kingdom

One Liberty Plaza, 20th Floor, New York, NY 10006, USA

477 Williamstown Road, Port Melbourne, VIC 3207, Australia

4843/24, 2nd Floor, Ansari Road, Daryaganj, Delhi – 110002, India

79 Anson Road, #06–04/06, Singapore 079906

Cambridge University Press is part of the University of Cambridge.

It furthers the University's mission by disseminating knowledge in the pursuit of education, learning and research at the highest international levels of excellence.

www.cambridge.org
Information on this title: www.cambridge.org/9780521315371

© Selection and notes Cambridge University Press 1985

First published 1985

40 39 38 37 36 35 34

Printed in Great Britain by CPI Group (UK) Ltd, Croydon CR04YY

A catalogue record for this publication is available from the British Library

ISBN 978-0-521-31537-1 Paperback

CONTENTS

TO THE READER

Nearly all the poems in this collection are poems which I have taught to students in their fourth and fifth years of secondary school. I have included poems which have been successful with the students. Not every poem has been successful with every student, but they have been successful with a large number of them.

What do I mean by successful? There are various ways of judging the success or otherwise of a poem you teach. Sometimes it is the animated manner in which the students talk about the poem during the lesson, which tells you they have responded well to it. Sometimes it is the ease with which they refer to parts of the poem in writing about it. Sometimes they make a kind of game during the year of quoting parts from a poem, or they might refer back to one poem while discussing another. It is easy to see in such cases that there is a positive delight in the poetry.

Given a choice of poems to write about in an essay, students, by the frequency of their selection of certain poems, indicate their favourites. Some poems inspire good creative writing, the students appearing to have immersed themselves in the original before turning out their own stories or poems based upon it. Occasionally students become very engrossed in reading the poem aloud in the class in various ways. And some poems become popular choices in the personal anthologies of a classful of students.

The six sections of this anthology are arranged to provide a mixture of styles and periods, but they are not thematically arranged. Whichever sections one reads, there will be a mixture of poems – longer and shorter, recent and long-established; poems which are directly accessible, and poems which require some probing thought and discussion before they can be fully apprehended.

This book also has several short sections about how to handle poetry for examinations in English Literature. This is because every student I have taught in the 14–16 age group has been preparing for an examination of some sort – whether the assessment has been made on course-work or by formal examination. It would be untrue to my own experience, therefore, if I ignored this factor in an anthology prepared for use in schools. This factor has never meant that the poetry has been less enjoyable; in fact, it is rather the reverse – students have found an extra stimulus in the fact that they have had a challenge to meet. It is

4

very much as if there has been, in a guaranteed audience for their efforts, an element added to the enjoyment of the poetry in itself. Of all the genres of English Literature I have had to teach to examination level, poetry has been the most fun, the most rewarding. It has offered more variety than a novel or a play, more complexity than short stories or essays; and has given less of a feeling of returning over the same ground than any other genre.

As a teacher, I have found that another advantage of the poem is the pleasure gained from a shared experience. I often feel that the only way to enjoy a novel is to read it alone at my own pace. But poetry, with its rhythmic emphasis, seems designed for reading aloud – for listening to as well as reading. All the poems in this collection are short enough to read aloud at a single sitting. And the compactness of a poem makes discussion, exploration, and explication a natural response.

For this reason there are no accompanying notes to individual poems. This is essentially an anthology to be shared by students and their teachers.

Poetry is literature at its best. Sometimes a poem is immediately enjoyable, delighting the reader through the impact which a particular combination of words can make. It reveals with a compact energy a startling insight, or expresses with a concise wit an idea which the reader has often had but never seen so perfectly presented. At other times a poem may be so delicate and subtle in working through a complex idea, that the reader has to read it several times before the ideas become thoroughly understood. This careful study of the poem can be an enjoyable challenge in itself. The feeling of elation once a complicated sequence of ideas has been mastered is often enough to make the more challenging poem the greater favourite in the end.

Jack Hydes

5

THE POEMS

Section C: 'Songs of other lands'

Section D: 'This changeful life'

Section E: 'Fill all fruit with ripeness to the core'

'Footprints in the dew'

Tall Nettles

Tall nettles cover up, as they have done
These many springs, the rusty harrow, the plough
Long worn out, and the roller made of stone:
Only the elm butt tops the nettles now.

This corner of the farmyard I like most:
As well as any bloom upon a flower
I like the dust on the nettles, never lost
Except to prove the sweetness of a shower.

Edward Thomas

Thistles

Against the rubber tongues of cows and the hoeing hands of
    men
Thistles spike the summer air
Or crackle open under a blue-black pressure.

Every one a revengeful burst
Of resurrection, a grasped fistful
Of splintered weapons and Icelandic frost thrust up

From the underground stain of a decayed Viking.
They are like pale hair and the gutturals of dialects.
Every one manages a plume of blood.

Then they grow grey, like men.
Mown down, it is a feud. Their sons appear,
Stiff with weapons, fighting back over the same ground.

Ted Hughes

Mushrooms

Overnight, very
Whitely, discreetly,
Very quietly

Our toes, our noses
Take hold on the loam,
Acquire the air.

Nobody sees us,
Stops us, betrays us;
The small grains make room.

Soft fists insist on   10
Heaving the needles,
The leafy bedding,

Even the paving.
Our hammers, our rams,
Earless and eyeless,

Perfectly voiceless,
Widen the crannies,
Shoulder through holes. We

Diet on water,
On crumbs of shadow,   20
Bland-mannered, asking

Little or nothing.
So many of us!
So many of us!

We are shelves, we are
Tables, we are meek,
We are edible,

Nudgers and shovers
In spite of ourselves.
Our kind multiplies: 30

We shall by morning
Inherit the earth.
Our foot's in the door.

Sylvia Plath

The Great Lover

I have been so great a lover: filled my days
So proudly with the splendour of Love's praise,
The pain, the calm, and the astonishment,
Desire illimitable, and still content,
And all dear names men use, to cheat despair,
For the perplexed and viewless streams that bear
Our hearts at random down the dark of life.
Now, ere the unthinking silence on that strife
Steals down, I would cheat drowsy Death so far,
My night shall be remembered for a star   10
That outshone all the suns of all men's days.
Shall I not crown them with immortal praise
Whom I have loved, who have given me, dared with me
High secrets, and in darkness knelt to see
The inenarrable godhead of delight?
Love is a flame: – we have beaconed the world's night.
A city: – and we have built it, these and I.
An emperor: – we have taught the world to die.
So, for their sakes I loved, ere I go hence,
And the high cause of Love's magnificence,   20
And to keep loyalties young, I'll write those names
Golden for ever, eagles, crying flames,
And set them as a banner, that men may know,
To dare the generations, burn, and blow
Out on the wind of Time, shining and streaming....

These I have loved:
               White plates and cups, clean-gleaming,
Ringed with blue lines; and feathery, faery dust;
Wet roofs, beneath the lamp-light; the strong crust
Of friendly bread; and many-tasting food;   30
Rainbows; and the blue bitter smoke of wood;
And radiant raindrops couching in cool flowers;
And flowers themselves, that sway through sunny hours,
Dreaming of moths that drink them under the moon;
Then, the cool kindliness of sheets, that soon
Smooth away trouble; and the rough male kiss
Of blankets; grainy wood; live hair that is
Shining and free; blue-massing clouds; the keen

Unpassioned beauty of a great machine;
The benison of hot water; furs to touch;   40
The good smell of old clothes; and others such –
The comfortable smell of friendly fingers,
Hair's fragrance, and the musty reek that lingers
About dead leaves and last year's ferns....
                                                    Dear names,
And thousand other throng to me! Royal flames;
Sweet water's dimpling laugh from tap or spring;
Holes in the ground; and voices that do sing;
Voices in laughter, too; and body's pain,
Soon turned to peace; and the deep-panting train;   50
Firm sands; the little dulling edge of foam
That browns and dwindles as the wave goes home;
And washen stones, gay for an hour; the cold
Graveness of iron; moist black earthen mould;
Sleep; and high places; footprints in the dew;
And oaks; and brown horse-chestnuts, glossy-new;
And new-peeled sticks; and shining pools on grass; –
All these have been my loves. And these shall pass,
Whatever passes not, in the great hour,
Nor all my passion, all my prayers, have power   60
To hold them with me through the gate of Death.
They'll play deserter, turn with the traitor breath,
Break the high bond we made, and sell Love's trust
And sacramented covenant to the dust.
– Oh, never a doubt but, somewhere, I shall wake,
And give what's left of love again, and make
New friends, now strangers....
                                        But the best I've known
Stays here, and changes, breaks, grows old, is blown
About the winds of the world, and fades from brains   70
Of living men, and dies.
                            Nothing remains.

O dear my loves, O faithless, once again
This one last gift I give: that after men
Shall know, and later lovers, far-removed,
Praise you, 'All these were lovely'; say, 'He loved.'

                                        Rupert Brooke

Rising Five

'I'm rising five', he said,
'Not four', and little coils of hair
Un-clicked themselves upon his head.
His spectacles, brimful of eyes to stare
At me and the meadow, reflected cones of light
Above his toffee-buckled cheeks. He'd been alive
Fifty-six months or perhaps a week more:
>   not four,
But rising five.

Around him in the field the cells of spring   10
Bubbled and doubled; buds unbuttoned; shoot
And stem shook out the creases from their frills,
And every tree was swilled with green.
It was the season after blossoming,
Before the forming of the fruit:
>   not May,
But rising June.

>   And in the sky
The dust dissected tangential light:
>   not day,   20
But rising night;
>   not now,
But rising soon.

The new buds push the old leaves from the bough.
We drop our youth behind us like a boy
Throwing away his toffee-wrappers. We never see the flower,
But only the fruit in the flower; never the fruit,
But only the rot in the fruit. We look for the marriage bed
In the baby's cradle, we look for the grave in the bed:
>   not living,   30
But rising dead.

Norman Nicholson

The Truly Great

I think continually of those who were truly great
Who, from the womb, remembered the soul's history
Through corridors of light where the hours are suns,
Endless and singing. Whose lovely ambition
Was that their lips, still touched with fire,
Should tell of the Spirit, clothed from head to foot in song.
And who hoarded from the Spring branches
The desires falling across their bodies like blossoms.

What is precious, is never to forget
The essential delight of the blood drawn from ageless springs   10
Breaking through rocks in worlds before our earth.
Never to deny its pleasure in the morning simple light
Nor its grave evening demand for love.
Never to allow gradually the traffic to smother
With noise and fog, the flowering of the Spirit.

Near the snow, near the sun, in the highest fields,
See how these names are fêted by the waving grass
And by the streamers of white cloud
And whispers of wind in the listening sky.
The names of those who in their lives fought for life,   20
Who wore at their hearts the fire's centre.
Born of the sun, they travelled a short while toward the sun
And left the vivid air signed with their honour.

Stephen Spender

16

Elegy Written in a Country Churchyard

The Curfew tolls the knell of parting day,
The lowing herd wind slowly o'er the lea,
The plowman homeward plods his weary way,
And leaves the world to darkness and to me.

Now fades the glimmering landscape on the sight,
And all the air a solemn stillness holds,
Save where the beetle wheels his droning flight,
And drowsy tinklings lull the distant folds;

Save that from yonder ivy-mantled tow'r
The mopeing owl does to the moon complain   10
Of such, as wand'ring near her secret bow'r,
Molest her ancient solitary reign.

Beneath those rugged elms, that yew-tree's shade,
Where heaves the turf in many a mould'ring heap,
Each in his narrow cell for ever laid,
The rude Forefathers of the hamlet sleep.

The breezy call of incense-breathing Morn,
The swallow twitt'ring from the straw-built shed,
The cock's shrill clarion, or the echoing horn,
No more shall rouse them from their lowly bed.   20

For them no more the blazing hearth shall burn,
Or busy housewife ply her evening care:
No children run to lisp their sire's return,
Or climb his knees the envied kiss to share.

Oft did the harvest to their sickle yield,
Their furrow oft the stubborn glebe has broke;
How jocund did they drive their team afield!
How bow'd the woods beneath their sturdy stroke!

Let not Ambition mock their useful toil,
Their homely joys, and destiny obscure;   30
Nor Grandeur hear with a disdainful smile,
The short and simple annals of the poor.

The boast of heraldry, the pomp of pow'r,
And all that beauty, all that wealth e'er gave,
Awaits alike th' inevitable hour.
The paths of glory lead but to the grave.

Nor you, ye Proud, impute to These the fault,
If Mem'ry o'er their Tomb no Trophies raise,
Where thro' the long-drawn isle and fretted vault
The pealing anthem swells the note of praise.   40

Can storied urn or animated bust
Back to its mansion call the fleeting breath?
Can Honour's voice provoke the silent dust,
Or Flatt'ry sooth the dull cold ear of Death?

Perhaps in this neglected spot is laid
Some heart once pregnant with celestial fire;
Hands, that the rod of empire might have sway'd,
Or wak'd to extasy the living lyre.

But Knowledge to their eyes her ample page
Rich with the spoils of time did ne'er unroll;   50
Chill Penury repress'd their noble rage,
And froze the genial current of the soul.

Full many a gem of purest ray serene,
The dark unfathom'd caves of ocean bear:
Full many a flower is born to blush unseen,
And waste its sweetness on the desert air.

Some village-Hampden, that with dauntless breast
The little Tyrant of his fields withstood;
Some mute inglorious Milton here may rest,
Some Cromwell guiltless of his country's blood.   60

Th'applause of list'ning senates to command,
The threats of pain and ruin to despise,
To scatter plenty o'er a smiling land,
And read their hist'ry in a nation's eyes,

Their lot forbad: nor circumscrib'd alone
Their growing virtues, but their crimes confin'd;
Forbad to wade through slaughter to a throne,
And shut the gates of mercy on mankind,

The struggling pangs of conscious truth to hide,
To quench the blushes of ingenuous shame,   70
Or heap the shrine of Luxury and Pride
With incense kindled at the Muse's flame.

Far from the madding crowd's ignoble strife,
Their sober wishes never learn'd to stray;
Along the cool sequester'd vale of life
They kept the noiseless tenor of their way.

Yet ev'n these bones from insult to protect
Some frail memorial still erected nigh,
With uncouth rhimes and shapeless sculpture deck'd,
Implores the passing tribute of a sigh.   80

Their name, their years, spelt by th' unlettered muse,
The place of fame and elegy supply:
And many a holy text around she strews,
That teach the rustic moralist to die.

For who to dumb Forgetfulness a prey,
This pleasing anxious being e'er resigned,
Left the warm precincts of the chearful day,
Nor cast one longing ling'ring look behind?

On some fond breast the parting soul relies,
Some pious drops the closing eye requires;   90
Ev'n from the tomb the voice of Nature cries,
Ev'n in our Ashes live their wonted Fires.

For thee, who mindful of th' unhonour'd Dead
Dost in these lines their artless tale relate;
If chance, by lonely contemplation led,
Some kindred Spirit shall inquire thy fate,

Haply some hoary-headed Swain may say,
'Oft have we seen him at the peep of dawn
Brushing with hasty steps the dews away
To meet the sun upon the upland lawn.   100

'There at the foot of yonder nodding beech
That wreathes its old fantastic roots so high,
His listless length at noontide would he stretch,
And pore upon the brook that babbles by.

'Hard by yon wood, now smiling as in scorn,
Mutt'ring his wayward fancies he would rove,
Now drooping, woeful wan, like one forlorn,
Or craz'd with care, or cross'd in hopeless love.

'One morn I miss'd him on the custom'd hill,
Along the heath and near his fav'rite tree;   110
Another came; nor yet beside the rill,
Nor up the lawn, nor at the wood was he;

'The next with dirges due in sad array
Slow thro' the church-way path we saw him borne.
Approach and read (for thou can'st read) the lay,
Grav'd on the stone beneath yon aged thorn.'

THE EPITAPH

Here rests his head upon the lap of Earth
A Youth to Fortune and to Fame unknown.
Fair Science frown'd not on his humble birth,
And Melancholy mark'd him for her own.   120

Large was his bounty, and his soul sincere,
Heav'n did a recompence as largely send:
He gave to Mis'ry all he had, a tear,
He gained from Heav'n ('twas all he wish'd) a friend.

No farther seek his merits to disclose,
Or draw his frailties from their dread abode,
(There they alike in trembling hope repose,)
The bosom of his Father and his God.

                                        Thomas Gray

Ozymandias

I met a traveller from an antique land
Who said: Two vast and trunkless legs of stone
Stand in the desert. Near them, on the sand,
Half sunk, a shattered visage lies, whose frown,
And wrinkled lip, and sneer of cold command
Tell that its sculptor well those passions read
Which yet survive (stamped on these lifeless things)
The hand that mocked them and the heart that fed:
And on the pedestal these words appear:
'My name is Ozymandias, king of kings:
Look on my works, ye Mighty, and despair!'
Nothing beside remains. Round the decay
Of that colossal wreck, boundless and bare
The lone and level sands stretch far away.

P. B. Shelley

Cold in the earth

Cold in the earth and the deep snow piled above thee!
Far, far removed, cold in the dreary grave!
Have I forgot, my Only Love, to love thee,
Severed at last by Time's all-wearing wave?

Now, when alone, do my thoughts no longer hover
Over the mountains on Angora's shore;
Resting their wings where heath and fern-leaves cover
That noble heart for ever, ever more?

Cold in the earth, and fifteen wild Decembers
From those brown hills have melted into spring –   10
Faithful indeed is the spirit that remembers
After such years of change and suffering!

Sweet Love of youth, forgive if I forget thee
While the World's tide is bearing me along:
Sterner desires and darker hopes beset me,
Hopes which obscure but cannot do thee wrong.

No other Sun has lightened up my heaven;
No other Star has ever shone for me:
All my life's bliss from thy dear life was given –
All my life's bliss is in the grave with thee.   20

But when the days of golden dreams had perished
And even Despair was powerless to destroy,
Then did I learn how existence could be cherished,
Strengthened and fed without the aid of joy.

Then did I check the tears of useless passion,
Weaned my young soul from yearning after thine;
Sternly denied its burning wish to hasten
Down to that tomb already more than mine!

And even yet, I dare not let it languish,
Dare not indulge in Memory's rapturous pain: 30
Once drinking deep of that divinest anguish,
How could I seek the empty world again?

Emily Brontë

The City of Orange Trees

'The city filled with orange trees
Is lost', which, interpreted, meant
All conspicuous luxuries
Augur ruinous punishment.

This fitted what he knew. The zeal
For conquest, prayer, decays; the child
Mocks pieties he cannot feel
And children's children are beguiled

By comfort, gardens, literature.
Aesthetics dazes them, safe lives   10
Grow lax and soon they can endure
No one but slaves, musicians, wives...

22

Till to degeneracy the Lord
Sends one who, like their forbears, spurns
Mere taste as mannered cant. The sword
Falls and the plundered city burns.

* * *

Heir to three generations' learning,
He closed his book, his masterpiece.
Silk rustled as he rose, turning,
Ready to parley now for peace   20

With one beyond the city gate
Who, barbarous, impatient, vain,
No vows or presents could placate –
The world-conqueror, Tamburlaine.

Dick Davis

Corpus Christi Carol

Lully, lulley, lully, lulley,
The faucon hath borne my mak away.

He bare hym up, he bare hym down,
He bare hym into an orchard brown.

In that orchard there was a hall,
That was hanged with purple and pall.

And in that hall there was a bede,
Hit was hanged with gold so rede.

And in that bed ther lythe a knyght,
His wounde bledyng day and nyght.

By that bedes side ther kneleth a may,
And she wepeth both night and day.

And by that beddes side ther stondeth a ston,
Corpus Christi wretyn theron.

Anonymous

Felix Randal

Felix Randal the farrier, O he is dead then? my duty all ended,
Who have watched his mould of man, big-boned and
  hardy-handsome
Pining, pining, till time when reason rambled in it and some
Fatal four disorders, fleshed there, all contended?

Sickness broke him. Impatient he cursed at first, but mended
Being anointed and all; though a heavenlier heart began some
Months earlier, since I had our sweet reprieve and ransom
Tendered to him. Ah well, God rest him all road ever he
  offended!

This seeing the sick endears them to us, us too it endears.
My tongue had taught thee comfort, touch had quenched thy
  tears,
Thy tears that touched my heart, child, Felix, poor Felix Randal;

How far from then forethought of, all thy more boisterous
  years,
When thou at the random grim forge, powerful amidst peers,
Didst fettle for the great grey drayhorse his bright and battering
  sandal!

Gerard Manley Hopkins

A Toccata of Galuppi's

I

Oh Galuppi, Baldassaro, this is very sad to find!
I can hardly misconceive you; it would prove me deaf and blind;
But although I take your meaning, 'tis with such a heavy mind!

II

Here you come with your old music, and here's all the good it
  brings.
What, they lived once thus at Venice where the merchants were
  the kings,
Where Saint Mark's is, where the Doges used to wed the sea
  with rings?

III

Ay, because the sea's the street there; and 't is arched by...what
  you call
...Shylock's bridge with houses on it, where they kept the
  carnival:
I was never out of England – it's as if I saw it all.

IV

Did young people take their pleasure when the sea was warm in
  May?   10
Balls and masks begun at midnight, burning ever to mid-day,
When they made up fresh adventures for the morrow, do you
  say?

V

Was a lady such a lady, cheeks so round and lips so red, –
On her neck the small face buoyant, like a bell-flower on its bed,
O'er the breast's superb abundance where a man might base his
  head?

VI

Well, and it was graceful of them – they'd break talk off and
  afford
– She, to bite her mask's black velvet – he, to finger on his
  sword,
While you sat and played Toccatas, stately at the clavichord?

VII

What? Those lesser thirds so plaintive, sixths diminished, sigh on
  sigh,
Told them something? Those suspensions, those solutions –
  'Must we die?'   20
Those commiserating sevenths – 'Life might last! we can but
  try!'

VIII

'Were you happy?' – 'Yes.' – 'And are you still as happy?' –
  'Yes. And you?'
– 'Then, more kisses!' – 'Did I stop them, when a million
  seemed so few?'
Hark, the dominant's persistence till it must be answered to!

IX

So, an octave struck the answer. Oh, they praised you, I dare
    say!
'Brave Galuppi! that was music! good alike at grave and gay!
'I can always leave off talking when I hear a master play!'

X

Then they left you for their pleasure: till in due time, one by
    one,
Some with lives that came to nothing, some with deeds as well
    undone,
Death stepped tacitly and took them where they never see the
    sun.   30

XI

But when I sit down to reason, think to take my stand nor
    swerve,
While I triumph o'er a secret wrung from nature's close reserve,
In you come with your cold music till I creep thro' every nerve.

XII

Yes, you, like a ghostly cricket, creaking where a house was
    burned:
'Dust and ashes, dead and done with, Venice spent what Venice
    earned.
'The soul, doubtless, is immortal – where a soul can be
    discerned.

XIII

'Yours for instance: you know physics, something of geology,
'Mathematics are your pastime; souls shall rise in their degree;
'Butterflies may dread extinction, – you'll not die, it cannot be!

XIV

'As for Venice and her people, merely born to bloom and drop,   40
'Here on earth they bore their fruitage, mirth and folly were the
    crop:
'What of soul was left, I wonder, when the kissing had to stop?

'Dust and ashes!' So you creak it, and I want the heart to scold.
Dear dead women, with such hair, too – what's become of all
  the gold
Used to hang and brush their bosoms? I feel chilly and grown
  old.
                                        Robert Browning

Piano and Drums

When at break of day at a riverside
I hear jungle drums telegraphing
the mystic rhythm, urgent, raw
like bleeding flesh, speaking of
primal youth and the beginning,
I see the panther ready to pounce,
the leopard snarling about to leap
and the hunters crouch with spears poised;

And my blood ripples, turns torrent,
topples the years and at once I'm   10
in my mother's laps a suckling;
at once I'm walking simple
paths with no innovations,
rugged, fashioned with the naked
warmth of hurrying feet and groping hearts
in green leaves and wild flowers pulsing.

Then I hear a wailing piano
solo speaking of complex ways
in tear-furrowed concerto;
of far away lands   20
and new horizons with
coaxing diminuendo, counterpoint,
crescendo. But lost in the labyrinth
of its complexities, it ends in the middle
of a phrase at a daggerpoint.

And I lost in the morning mist
of an age at a riverside keep
wandering in the mystic rhythm
of jungle drums and the concerto.

                    Gabriel Okara

The Wild Swans at Coole

The trees are in their autumn beauty,
The woodland paths are dry,
Under the October twilight the water
Mirrors a still sky;
Upon the brimming water among the stones
Are nine-and-fifty swans.

The nineteenth autumn has come upon me
Since I first made my count;
I saw, before I had well finished,
All suddenly mount   10
And scatter wheeling in great broken rings
Upon their clamorous wings.

I have looked upon those brilliant creatures,
And now my heart is sore.
All's changed since I, hearing at twilight,
The first time on this shore,
The bell-beat of their wings above my head,
Trod with a lighter tread.

Unwearied still, lover by lover,
They paddle in the cold   20
Companionable streams or climb the air;
Their hearts have not grown old;
Passion and conquest, wander where they will,
Attend upon them still.

But now they drift on the still water,
Mysterious, beautiful;
Among what rushes will they build,
By what lake's edge or pool
Delight men's eyes when I awake some day
To find they have flown away?   30

W. B. Yeats

Afterwards

When the Present has latched its postern behind my tremulous
    stay,
And the May month flaps its glad green leaves like wings,
Delicate-filmed as new-spun silk, will the neighbours say,
    'He was a man who used to notice such things'?

If it be in the dusk when, like an eyelid's soundless blink,
    The dewfall-hawk comes crossing the shades to alight
Upon the wind-warped upland thorn, a gazer may think,
    'To him this must have been a familiar sight.'

If I pass during some nocturnal blackness, mothy and warm,
    When the hedgehog travels furtively over the lawn,   10
One may say, 'He strove that such innocent creatures should
    come to no harm,
    But he could do little for them; and now he is gone.'

If, when hearing that I have been stilled at last, they stand at
    the door,
    Watching the full-starred heavens that winter sees,
Will this thought rise on those who will meet my face no more,
    'He was one who had an eye for such mysteries'?

And will any say when my bell of quittance is heard in the
    gloom,
    And a crossing breeze cuts a pause in its outrollings,
Till they rise again, as they were a new bell's boom,
    'He hears it not now, but used to notice such things'?   20

Thomas Hardy

Solitude

Laugh, and the world laughs with you;
    Weep, and you weep alone;
For the sad old earth must borrow its mirth,
    But has trouble enough of its own.
Sing, and the hills will answer;
    Sigh, it is lost on the air;
The echoes bound to a joyful sound,
    But shrink from voicing care.

Rejoice, and men will seek you;
    Grieve, and they turn and go;   10
They want full measure of all your pleasure,
    But they do not need your woe.
Be glad, and your friends are many;
    Be sad, and you lose them all, –
There are none to decline your nectared wine,
    But alone you must drink life's gall.

Feast, and your halls are crowded;
    Fast, and the world goes by.
Succeed and give, and it helps you live,
    But no man can help you die.   20
For there is room in the halls of pleasure
    For a large and lordly train,
But one by one we must all file on
    Through the narrow aisles of pain.

Ella Wheeler Wilcox

The Early Purges

I was six when I first saw kittens drown.
Dan Taggart pitched them, 'the scraggy wee shits',
Into a bucket; a frail metal sound,

Soft paws scraping like mad. But their tiny din
Was soon soused. They were slung on the snout
Of the pump and the water pumped in.

'Sure isn't it better for them now?' Dan said.
Like wet gloves they bobbed and shone till he sluiced
Them out on the dunghill, glossy and dead.

Suddenly frightened, for days I sadly hung   10
Round the yard, watching the three sogged remains
Turn mealy and crisp as old summer dung

Until I forgot them. But the fear came back
When Dan trapped big rats, snared rabbits, shot crows
Or, with a sickening tug, pulled old hens' necks.

Still, living displaces false sentiments
And now, when shrill pups are prodded to drown
I just shrug, 'Bloody pups'. It makes sense:

'Prevention of cruelty' talk cuts ice in town
Where they consider death unnatural,   20
But on well-run farms pests have to be kept down.

Seamus Heaney

A Valediction: Forbidding Mourning

As virtuous men passe mildly away,
    And whisper to their soules, to goe,
Whilst some of their sad friends doe say,
    The breath goes now, and some say, no:

So let us melt, and make no noise,
    No teare-floods, nor sigh-tempests move,
T'were prophanation of our joyes
    To tell the layetie our love.

Moving of th'earth brings harmes and feares,
    Men reckon what it did and meant,   10
But trepidation of the spheares,
    Though greater farre, is innocent.

Dull sublunary lovers love
    (Whose soule is sense) cannot admit
Absence, because it doth remove
    Those things which elemented it.

But we by a love, so much refin'd,
    That our selves know not what it is,
Inter-assured of the mind,
    Care lesse, eyes, lips, and hands to misse.   20

Our two soules therefore, which are one,
    Though I must goe, endure not yet
A breach, but an expansion,
    Like gold to ayery thinnesse beate.

If they be two, they are two so
    As stiffe twin compasses are two,
Thy soule the fixt foot, makes no show
    To move, but doth, if th'other doe.

And though it in the center sit,
    Yet when the other far doth rome,   30
It leanes, and hearkens after it,
    And growes erect, as that comes home.

Such wilt thou be to mee, who must
  Like th'other foot, obliquely runne;
Thy firmnes drawes my circle just,
  And makes me end, where I begunne.

John Donne

The Telephone

'When I was just as far as I could walk
From here today,
There was an hour
All still
When leaning with my head against a flower
I heard you talk.
Don't say I didn't, for I heard you say –
You spoke from that flower on the window sill –
Do you remember what it was you said?'

'First tell me what it was you thought you heard.'

'Having found the flower and driven a bee away,
I leaned my head,
And holding by the stalk,
I listened and I thought I caught the word –
What was it? Did you call me by my name?
Or did you say –
Someone said "Come" – I heard it as I bowed.'

'I may have thought as much, but not aloud.'

'Well, so I came.'

Robert Frost

Telephone Conversation

The price seemed reasonable, location
Indifferent. The landlady swore she lived
Off premises. Nothing remained
But self-confession. 'Madam,' I warned,
'I hate a wasted journey – I am African.'
Silence. Silenced transmission of
Pressurized good-breeding. Voice, when it came,
Lipstick coated, long gold-rolled
Cigarette-holder pipped. Caught I was, foully.
'HOW DARK?'...I had not misheard...'ARE YOU LIGHT   10
OR VERY DARK?' Button B. Button A. Stench
Of rancid breath of public hide-and-speak.
Red booth. Red pillar-box. Red double-tiered
Omnibus squelching tar. It *was* real! Shamed
By ill-mannered silence, surrender
Pushed dumbfoundment to beg simplification.
Considerate she was, varying the emphasis –
'ARE YOU DARK? OR VERY LIGHT?' Revelation came.
'You mean – like plain or milk chocolate?'
Her assent was clinical, crushing in its light   20
Impersonality. Rapidly, wave-length adjusted,
I chose. 'West African sepia' – and as afterthought,
'Down in my passport.' Silence for spectroscopic
Flight of fancy, till truthfulness clanged her accent
Hard on the mouthpiece. 'WHAT'S THAT?' conceding
'DON'T KNOW WHAT THAT IS.' 'Like brunette.'
'THAT'S DARK, ISN'T IT?' 'Not altogether.
Facially, I am brunette, but, madam, you should see
The rest of me. Palm of my hand, soles of my feet
Are a peroxide blond. Friction, caused –   30
Foolishly, madam – by sitting down, has turned
My bottom raven black – One moment, madam!' – sensing
Her receiver rearing on the thunderclap
About my ears – 'Madam,' I pleaded, 'wouldn't you rather
See for yourself?'

Wole Soyinka

Look, stranger, at this island now

Look, stranger, at this island now
The leaping light for your delight discovers,
Stand stable here
And silent be,
That through the channels of the ear
May wander like a river
The swaying sound of the sea.

Here at the small field's ending pause
Where the chalk wall falls to the foam, and its tall ledges
Oppose the pluck   10
And knock of the tide,
And the shingle scrambles after the suck-
ing surf, and the gull lodges
A moment on its sheer side.

Far off like floating seeds the ships
Diverge on urgent voluntary errands;
And the full view
Indeed may enter
And move in memory as now these clouds do,
That pass the harbour mirror   20
And all the summer through the waters saunter.

W. H. Auden

WRITING ESSAYS ON POETRY FOR EXAMINATIONS

In examinations you are usually required to write an essay which presents an argument in response to a particular question. Unless the poem is actually printed on the examination paper, you will be awarded marks for recalling from memory relevant quotations to support your argument. The typical division of marks in such examinations is:

> knowledge of the text – 10
> answering the question – 10
> response to the text – 10
> Total – 30

You will notice that a good knowledge of the text, on its own will not give you enough marks to pass. And although you would gain a good pass if you had a good knowledge of the text and answered the question set, you would not gain enough marks for a distinction (grade A), which is usually about 70%. In fact it is difficult to perform well in the first two aspects without showing a positive response to the text. We can briefly look at each of these three elements in turn – knowledge of the text, answering the question, response to the text.

Knowledge of the text

You might well, during the course of your studies, find that you wish to learn poems by heart. But this is not the only way to acquire a knowledge of the text. The best way to familiarize yourself with the poems you study is to read carefully through them, selecting quotations for the essays you have to write during your course. You will probably find that some quotations are useful in several contexts, so that repeated use will make you familiar with them. It is helpful to write down quotations in your practice essays by taking in a whole line or sentence at a time, rather than looking up at the text for each single word.

In examinations you will find that the shorter a quotation is, the better. It is a waste of time to write out a whole eight-line stanza of a poem to prove a point in your argument when three words from that stanza would have been sufficient to make the point.

Answering the question

If you are being asked to write an essay on a poem, the only way anyone can find out what you think about the poem is to ask for your opinion in a form which will require you to organize it in your own way. Otherwise, you could simply reproduce the words of somebody else, such as your teacher. A teacher's thoughts only become the legitimate ideas of a student once the student has assimilated them so thoroughly that she or he can command them in a variety of contexts, selecting from them and using them as appropriate.

Consequently, anything you write in your essay which the question has not asked for will at best be ignored, and in the worst case it will show that you have not sufficiently understood the poem to be able to discuss it from various angles. You might not lose marks directly for irrelevance, but you will be penalizing yourself by wasting time on writing something that will not help you in any way.

It is for this reason that time spent in planning your answer, in considering what points you will make to answer the particular question, is not wasted. You are far more likely to waste time by plunging straight into your answer without careful consideration of what is required of you.

Response to the text

This element is the most difficult to speak of in isolation. English Literature is a subject which aims not only at the acquisition of knowledge and the development of logical thinking, but also at the education of taste.

Nobody can select a poem for an anthology that will be well liked by everybody, but any poem chosen will have some merit in it. What can appear an uninviting text at a first reading, will often become a rewarding experience once you know more about it and begin to think and talk about it. It is as if further familiarity with texts makes them more appealing. This could be because they become part of your own thinking. Or it might be because certain difficulties are only a matter of strangeness; they disappear once the text is no longer strange.

Don't be determined to say whether you like a poem or not. Concentrate rather on showing your awareness of what the author is saying. Relate the author's points to what the question asks you about. If in the course of your essay you quote – or closely echo – the author's own words in relevant contexts, the blending of your own thoughts with those of the author will show a sensitivity to the text. This is what is meant by response.

An example will help. Read the poem printed on the next page and then look at the commentaries written by two students.

The Sick Rose

O Rose, thou art sick!
The invisible worm
That flies in the night,
In the howling storm,

Has found out thy bed
Of crimson joy:
And his dark secret love
Does thy life destroy.

William Blake

(A) Blake's poem called 'The Sick Rose' is a good example of the cruelty of nature. The worm destroys the beautiful rose, eating through its petals. The rose has no defence against the worm since the worm is invisible and flies in the night. The poem is very short – only eight lines long, but it is very effective.

(B) In 'The Sick Rose' Blake presents the indifference of the world to ideas of justice. The lines are very short and brutal. Even the opening line seems callous: 'O Rose, thou art sick!' The rest of the poem is a single sentence which says in very simple language that the worm has destroyed it. The language is simple because the act is a simple everyday act. Yet because the rose is addressed like a person we feel sorry for it and feel that the worm is treacherous because it is invisible and 'flies in the night'. Yet the worm is attracted to the rose like a lover, and in taking refuge from the 'howling storm' is itself a kind of victim of the forces of nature. The fact that his 'love' destroys the rose is another example of the incompatibility of the world's creatures. This is one of Blake's most unpleasant poems.

Which of the two passages shows the better response to Blake's poem? Ignoring the different lengths of the passages, say why you think one shows more response than the other.

'The light of setting suns'

Two Look at Two

Love and forgetting might have carried them
A little further up the mountainside
With night so near, but not much further up.
They must have halted soon in any case
With thoughts of the path back, how rough it was
With rock and washout, and unsafe in darkness;
When they were halted by a tumbled wall
With barbed-wire binding. They stood facing this,
Spending what onward impulse they still had
In one last look the way they must not go,   10
On up the failing path, where, if a stone
Or earthslide moved at night, it moved itself;
No footstep moved it. 'This is all,' they sighed,
'Good-night to woods.' But not so; there was more.
A doe from round a spruce stood looking at them
Across the wall, as near the wall as they.
She saw them in their field, they her in hers.
The difficulty of seeing what stood still,
Like some up-ended boulder split in two,
Was in her clouded eyes: they saw no fear there.   20
She seemed to think that, two thus, they were safe.
Then, as if they were something that, though strange,
She could not trouble her mind with too long,
She sighed and passed unscared along the wall.
'This, then, is all. What more is there to ask?'
But no, not yet. A snort to bid them wait.
A buck from round the spruce stood looking at them
Across the wall, as near the wall as they.
This was an antlered buck of lusty nostril,
Not the same doe come back into her place.   30
He viewed them quizzically with jerks of head,
As if to ask, 'Why don't you make some motion?

Or give some sign of life? Because you can't.
I doubt if you're as living as you look.'
Thus till he had them almost feeling dared
To stretch a proffering hand – and a spell-breaking.
Then he too passed unscared along the wall.
Two had seen two, whichever side you spoke from.
'This *must* be all.' It was all. Still they stood,
A great wave from it going over them,   40
As if the earth in one unlooked-for favour
Had made them certain earth returned their love.

Robert Frost

Mountain Lion

Climbing through the January snow, into the Lobo canyon
Dark grow the spruce-trees, blue is the balsam, water sounds
    still unfrozen, and the trail is still evident.

Men!
Two men!
Men! The only animal in the world to fear!

They hesitate.
We hesitate.
They have a gun.
We have no gun.

Then we all advance, to meet.   10

Two Mexicans, strangers, emerging out of the dark and snow
    and inwardness of the Lobo valley.
What are you doing here on this vanishing trail?

What is he carrying?
Something yellow.
A deer?

Qué tiene, amigo?
León –

He smiles, foolishly, as if he were caught doing wrong.
And we smile, foolishly, as if we didn't know.
He is quite gentle and dark-faced.   20

It is a mountain lion,
A long, long slim cat, yellow like a lioness.
Dead.
He trapped her this morning, he says, smiling foolishly.

Lift up her face,
Her round, bright face, bright as frost.
Her round, fine-fashioned head, with two dead ears;
And stripes in the brilliant frost of her face, sharp, fine dark
    rays,
Dark, keen, fine eyes in the brilliant frost of her face.
Beautiful dead eyes.   30

Hermoso es!

They go out towards the open;
We go on into the gloom of Lobo.
And above the trees I found her lair,
A hole in the blood-orange brilliant rocks that stick up, a little
    cave.
And bones, and twigs, and a perilous ascent.

So, she will never leap up that way again, with the yellow flash
    of a mountain lion's long shoot!
And her bright striped frost-face will never watch any more, out
    of the shadow of the cave in the blood-orange rock,
Above the trees of the Lobo dark valley-mouth!

Instead, I look out.   40
And out to the dim of the desert, like a dream, never real;

To the snow of the Sangre de Cristo mountains, the ice of the
    mountains of Picoris,
And near across at the opposite steep of snow, green trees
    motionless standing in snow, like a Christmas toy.

And I think in this empty world there was room for me and a
mountain lion.
And I think in the world beyond, how easily we might spare a
million or two of humans
And never miss them.
Yet what a gap in the world, the missing white frost-face of that
slim yellow mountain lion!

D. H. Lawrence

Musée des Beaux Arts

About suffering they were never wrong,
The Old Masters: how well they understood
Its human position; how it takes place
While someone else is eating or opening a window or just
    walking dully along;
How, when the aged are reverently, passionately waiting
For the miraculous birth, there always must be
Children who did not specially want it to happen, skating
On a pond at the edge of the wood:
They never forgot
That even the dreadful martyrdom must run its course   10
Anyhow in a corner, some untidy spot
Where the dogs go on with their doggy life and the torturer's
    horse
Scratches its innocent behind on a tree.

In Brueghel's *Icarus*, for instance: how everything turns away
Quite leisurely from the disaster; the ploughman may
Have heard the splash, the forsaken cry,
But for him it was not an important failure; the sun shone
As it had to on the white legs disappearing into the green
Water; and the expensive delicate ship that must have seen
Something amazing, a boy falling out of the sky,   20
Had somewhere to get to and sailed calmly on.

W. H. Auden

The Fallen Birdman

The oldman in the cripplechair
Died in transit through the air
And slopped into the road.

The driver of the lethallorry
Trembled out and cried: 'I'm sorry,
But it was his own fault'.

Humans snuggled round the mess
In masochistic tenderness
As raindrops danced in his womb.

*   *   *

But something else obsessed my brain,
The canvas, twistedsteel and cane,
His chair, spreadeagled in the rain,
Like a fallen birdman.

Roger McGough

The Porpoises

Plutarch would have called it suicide,
some strange ancestral yearning of the school
that drove them to the harbour, past the bar,
then left them, beached and squealing, on the rocks,
abandoned by the quick ebb of the tide
that slides out through the darkness. Here they lay,
bleeding, overheating, as their calls
went whistling to each other through the sea,
the free ones swimming back towards the lost
till they in turn were stranded, and the men   10
came wading from the village, torches high
to finish them with cleavers. After all,
such creatures were the gift of Providence,
pig-fish from the ocean, porpoises,
their blunt heads and their countershaded sides
sent in to feed the village. That they lived

as harmless as young children on the deep,
would court the running hull upon the foam,
rush at it head on, to rub its sides
with amorous rough vigour – fawned on men,   20
and lifted them from drowning in the waves,
mourned in deep affliction if they died,
was scarcely to the point. Life was hard,
the women three parts starving, and the beasts
condemned to die, exhausted, by their own
irrational compulsion. Nonetheless
the sheer fact of their killing seems a crime,
intrudes on my awareness every time
I think upon creation, on its Cause,
that link with mutilation that distorts   30
the bond of pure dependence: and at dusk,
especially when the blue gloss of the mud
thrusts up above the grey silt of the tide
I feel myself accused, and in my mind
act out my reparation. Drag them down,
haul them by the tail-flukes or the snout
towards the deeper water: hold them up,
their skin as tough as rubber, smooth as wrack,
the warm air of their blowholes on my arms,
until, their strength returning, off they plunge   40
in great leaps past the headland. Watch them go,
the slow heave of their undulating backs
departing like a groundswell through the waves
in synchronised perfection, till they float
at rest beneath the moonlight, with each head
a map of echo-shadows, as they hang
transparent to the uproar of the deep.

John Gurney

The Pond

There were no willows but there was a pond
Steep at the edges where I sat and stared
Past my reflection, deep into seeming light.

As I grew older, so the carp grew large,
Green among weed or gold, or turned
A silver belly up; in autumn brisk,

While in the summer they lay stunned, inert.
A child might drown in such a pond, I heard.
Watching there, for a time I was a child.

One summer it was hot for days and days.   10
Green skin spread on the water, water-weed
Broke through the surface, and at last the bed

Began to parch, what little damp remained
Was stagnant and then mud in which the fish
Pulsed gracelessly, snared like wingless birds.

No more reflections then: I walked among
The large fish that for years had drawn my eye
And saw them take the air to heart, and how

They urged their bodies under the wilted weeds
And died. Incurious birds   20
Dropped from the air among them, finding food.

Too late the rain came, and I saw my face
Again on water, rippled by a breeze
Or on calm days whole and staring deep

Where water-weed revived but wore a light
Now literal and creatureless.
In such a pond a child might drown.

                                    Michael Schmidt

Motorcycle Irene

There she sits a'-smokin'
Reefer in her mouth.
Her hair hanging northward
As she travels south.
Dirty, on her Harley,
(But her nails are clean.)
Super-powered, de-flowered,
Over-eighteen Irene.

I've seen her in the bare
Where her tattoos and her chains   10
Wrap around her body,
Where written are the names
Of prisons she's been in,
and lovers she has seen,
Curve-winding, bumping, grinding
Motorcycle Irene.

Ground round like hamburger
Laying in a splat
'Tis Irene, her sheen I seen
In pieces crumpled flat.   20
Her feet were in the bushes,
Her toes were in her hat,
Stark-ravin', un-shaven
Motorcycle Irene.

The Hunchback, the Cripple,
The Horseman and the Fool,
Prayer books and candles, and
Carpets cloaks and jewels,
Knowing all the answers
Breaking all the rules,   30
With stark naked, unsacred,
Motorcycle Irene.

Skip Spence

The Toys

My little Son, who look'd from thoughtful eyes
And moved and spoke in quiet grown-up wise,
Having my law the seventh time disobey'd,
I struck him, and dismiss'd
With hard words and unkiss'd,
His Mother, who was patient, being dead.
Then, fearing lest his grief should hinder sleep,
I visited his bed,
But found him slumbering deep,
With darken'd eyelids, and their lashes yet   10
From his late sobbing wet.
And I, with moan,
Kissing away his tears, left others of my own;
For, on a table drawn beside his head,
He had put, within his reach,
A box of counters and a red-vein'd stone,
A piece of glass abraded by the beach
And six or seven shells,
A bottle with bluebells
And two French copper coins, ranged there with careful art,   20
To comfort his sad heart.
So when that night I pray'd
To God, I wept, and said:
Ah, when at last we lie with tranced breath,
Not vexing Thee in death,
And Thou rememberest of what toys
We made our joys,
How weakly understood,
Thy great commanded good,
Then, fatherly not less   30
Than I whom Thou hast moulded from the clay,
Thou'lt leave Thy wrath, and say,
'I will be sorry for their childishness.'

Coventry Patmore

47

Little Boy Crying

Your mouth contorting in brief spite and
Hurt, your laughter metamorphosed into howls,
Your frame so recently relaxed now tight
With three-year-old frustration, your bright eyes
Swimming tears, splashing your bare feet,
You stand there angling for a moment's hint
Of guilt or sorrow for the quick slap struck.

The ogre towers above you, that grim giant,
Empty of feeling, a colossal cruel,
Soon victim of the tale's conclusion, dead   10
At last. You hate him, you imagine
Chopping clean the tree he's scrambling down
Or plotting deeper pits to trap him in.

You cannot understand, not yet,
The hurt your easy tears can scald him with,
Nor guess the wavering hidden behind that mask.
This fierce man longs to lift you, curb your sadness
With piggy-back or bull-fight, anything,
But dare not ruin the lessons you should learn.

You must not make a plaything of the rain.   20

Mervyn Morris

Nursery Rhyme of Innocence and Experience

I had a silver penny
   And an apricot tree
And I said to the sailor
   On the white quay

'Sailor O sailor
   Will you bring me
If I give you my penny
   And my apricot tree

'A fez from Algeria
   An Arab drum to beat   10
A little gilt sword
   And a parakeet?'

And he smiled and he kissed me
   As strong as death
And I saw his red tongue
   And I felt his sweet breath

'You may keep your penny
  And your apricot tree
And I'll bring your presents
  Back from sea.'   20

O, the ship dipped down
  On the rim of the sky
And I waited while three
  Long summers went by

Then one steel morning
  On the white quay
I saw a grey ship
  Come in from sea

Slowly she came
  Across the bay   30
For her flashing rigging
  Was shot away

All round her wake
  The seabirds cried
And flew in and out
  Of the hole in her side

Slowly she came
  In the path of the sun
And I heard the sound
  Of a distant gun   40

And a stranger came running
  Up to me
From the deck of the ship
  And he said, said he

'O are you the boy
  Who would wait on the quay
With the silver penny
  And the apricot tree?

'I've a plum-coloured fez
  And a drum for thee   50
And a sword and a parakeet
  From over the sea.'

'O where is the sailor
  With bold red hair?
And what is that volley
  On the bright air?

'O where are the other
  Girls and boys?
And why have you brought me
  Children's toys?'   60

Charles Causley

49

My Last Duchess

That's my last Duchess painted on the wall,
Looking as if she were alive. I call
That piece a wonder, now: Frà Pandolf's hands
Worked busily a day, and there she stands.
Will 't please you sit and look at her? I said
'Frà Pandolf' by design, for never read
Strangers like you that pictured countenance,
The depth and passion of its earnest glance,
But to myself they turned (since none puts by
The curtain I have drawn for you, but I)   10
And seemed as they would ask me, if they durst,
How such a glance came there; so, not the first
Are you to turn and ask thus. Sir, 't was not
Her husband's presence only, called that spot
Of joy into the Duchess' cheek: perhaps
Frà Pandolf chanced to say 'Her mantle laps
'Over my lady's wrist too much,' or 'Paint
'Must never hope to reproduce the faint
'Half-flush that dies along her throat:' such stuff
Was courtesy, she thought, and cause enough   20
For calling up that spot of joy. She had
A heart – how shall I say? – too soon made glad,
Too easily impressed; she liked whate'er
She looked on, and her looks went everywhere.
Sir, 't was all one! My favour at her breast,
The dropping of the daylight in the West,
The bough of cherries some officious fool
Broke in the orchard for her, the white mule
She rode with round the terrace – all and each
Would draw from her alike the approving speech,   30
Or blush, at least. She thanked men, – good! but thanked
Somehow – I know not how – as if she ranked
My gift of a nine-hundred-years-old name
With anybody's gift. Who'd stoop to blame
This sort of trifling? Even had you skill
In speech – (which I have not) – to make your will
Quite clear to such an one, and say, 'Just this
'Or that in you disgusts me; here you miss,
'Or there exceed the mark' – and if she let

Herself be lessoned so, nor plainly set   40
Her wits to yours, forsooth, and made excuse,
– E'en then would be some stooping; and I choose
Never to stoop. Oh sir, she smiled, no doubt,
Whene'er I passed her; but who passed without
Much the same smile? This grew; I gave commands;
Then all smiles stopped together. There she stands
As if alive. Will 't please you rise? We'll meet
The company below, then. I repeat,
The Count your master's known munificence
Is ample warrant that no just pretence   50
Of mine for dowry will be disallowed;
Though his fair daughter's self, as I avowed
At starting, is my object. Nay, we'll go
Together down, sir. Notice Neptune, though,
Taming a sea-horse, thought a rarity,
Which Claus of Innsbruck cast in bronze for me!

Robert Browning

Mariana

'Mariana in the moated grange.' *Measure for Measure*

With blackest moss the flower-plots
    Were thickly crusted, one and all:
The rusted nails fell from the knots
    That held the pear to the gable-wall.
The broken sheds look'd sad and strange:
    Unlifted was the clinking latch;
    Weeded and worn the ancient thatch
Upon the lonely moated grange.
        She only said, 'My life is dreary,
        He cometh not,' she said;   10
    She said, 'I am aweary, aweary,
        I would that I were dead!'

Her tears fell with the dews at even;
  Her tears fell ere the dews were dried;
She could not look on the sweet heaven,
  Either at morn or eventide.
After the flitting of the bats,
  When thickest dark did trance the sky,
  She drew her casement-curtain by,
And glanced athwart the glooming flats.   20
    She only said, 'The night is dreary,
      He cometh not,' she said;
    She said, 'I am aweary, aweary,
      I would that I were dead!'

Upon the middle of the night,
  Waking she heard the night-fowl crow;
The cock sung out an hour ere light:
  From the dark fen the oxen's low
Came to her: without hope of change,
  In sleep she seem'd to walk forlorn,   30
  Till cold winds woke the gray-eyed morn
About the lonely moated grange.
    She only said, 'The day is dreary,
      He cometh not,' she said;
    She said, 'I am aweary, aweary,
      I would that I were dead!'

About a stone-cast from the wall
  A sluice with blacken'd waters slept,
And o'er it many, round and small,
  The cluster'd marish-mosses crept.   40
Hard by a poplar shook alway,
  All silver-green with gnarled bark:
  For leagues no other tree did mark
The level waste, the rounding gray.
    She only said, 'My life is dreary,
      He cometh not,' she said;
    She said, 'I am aweary, aweary,
      I would that I were dead!'

And ever when the moon was low,
   And the shrill winds were up and away,   50
In the white curtain, to and fro,
   She saw the gusty shadow sway.
But when the moon was very low,
   And wild winds bound within their cell,
   The shadow of the poplar fell
Upon her bed, across her brow.
      She only said, 'The night is dreary,
         He cometh not,' she said;
      She said, 'I am aweary, aweary,
         I would that I were dead!'   60

All day within the dreamy house,
   The doors upon their hinges creak'd;
The blue fly sung in the pane; the mouse
   Behind the mouldering wainscot shriek'd,
Or from the crevice peer'd about.
   Old faces glimmer'd thro' the doors,
   Old footsteps trod the upper floors,
Old voices called her from without.
      She only said, 'My life is dreary,
         He cometh not,' she said;   70
      She said, 'I am aweary, aweary,
         I would that I were dead!'

The sparrow's chirrup on the roof,
   The slow clock ticking, and the sound
Which to the wooing wind aloof
   The poplar made, did all confound
Her sense; but most she loathed the hour
   When the thick-moted sunbeam lay
   Athwart the chambers, and the day
Was sloping toward his western bower.   80
      Then, said she, 'I am very dreary,
         He will not come,' she said;
      She wept, 'I am aweary, aweary,
         Oh God, that I were dead!'

Alfred, Lord Tennyson

The Voice

Woman much missed, how you call to me, call to me,
Saying that now you are not as you were
When you have changed from the one who was all to me,
But as at first, when our day was fair.

Can it be you that I hear? Let me view you, then,
Standing as when I drew near to the town
Where you would wait for me: yes, as I knew you then,
Even to the original air-blue gown!

Or is it only the breeze, in its listlessness
Travelling across the wet mead to me here,
You being ever dissolved to wan wistlessness,
Heard no more again far or near?

Thus I; faltering forward,
Leaves around me falling,
Wind oozing thin through the thorn from norward,
And the woman calling.

Thomas Hardy

A nocturnall upon S. Lucies day,
Being the shortest day

Tis the yeares midnight, and it is the dayes,
Lucies, who scarce seaven houres herself unmaskes,
    The Sunne is spent, and now his flasks
    Send forth light squibs, no constant rayes;
        The worlds whole sap is sunke:
The generall balme th'hydroptique earth hath drunk,
Whither, as to the beds-feet, life is shrunke,
Dead and enterr'd; yet all these seeme to laugh,
Compar'd with mee, who am their Epitaph.

Study me then, you who shall lovers bee   10
At the next world, that is, at the next Spring:
    For I am every dead thing,
    In whom love wrought new Alchimie.
        For his art did expresse
A quintessence even from nothingnesse,
From dull privations, and leane emptinesse:
He ruin'd mee, and I am re-begot
Of absence, darknesse, death; things which are not.

All others, from all things, draw all that's good,
Life, soule, forme, spirit, whence they beeing have;   20
    I, by loves limbecke, am the grave
    Of all, that's nothing. Oft a flood
        Have wee two wept, and so
Drownd the whole world, us two; oft did we grow
To be two Chaosses, when we did show
Care to ought else; and often absences
Withdrew our soules, and made us carcasses.

But I am by her death, (which word wrongs her)
Of the first nothing, the Elixer grown;
    Were I a man, that I were one,   30
    I needs must know; I should preferre,
        If I were any beast,
Some ends, some means; Yea plants, yea stones detest,
And love; All, all some properties invest;
If I an ordinary nothing were,
As shadow, a light, and body must be here.

But I am None; nor will my Sunne renew.
You lovers, for whose sake, the lesser Sunne
    At this time to the Goat is runne
    To fetch new lust, and give it you,   40
        Enjoy your summer all;
Since shee enjoyes her long nights festivall,
Let mee prepare towards her, and let mee call
This houre her Vigill, and her Eve, since this
Both the yeares, and the dayes deep midnight is.

                                    John Donne

Lines

Composed a few miles above Tintern Abbey

Five years have past; five summers, with the length
Of five long winters! and again I hear
These waters, rolling from their mountain-springs
With a soft inland murmur. – Once again
Do I behold these steep and lofty cliffs,
That on a wild secluded scene impress
Thoughts of more deep seclusion; and connect
The landscape with the quiet of the sky.
The day is come when I again repose
Here, under this dark sycamore, and view   10
These plots of cottage-ground, these orchard-tufts,
Which at this season, with their unripe fruits,
Are clad in one green hue, and lose themselves
'Mid groves and copses. Once again I see
These hedge-rows, hardly hedge-rows, little lines
Of sportive wood run wild: these pastoral farms,
Green to the very door; and wreaths of smoke
Sent up, in silence, from among the trees!
With some uncertain notice, as might seem
Of vagrant dwellers in the houseless woods,   20
Or of some Hermit's cave, where by his fire
The Hermit sits alone.
                            These beauteous forms,
Through a long absence, have not been to me
As is a landscape to a blind man's eye:
But oft, in lonely rooms, and 'mid the din
Of towns and cities, I have owed to them,
In hours of weariness, sensations sweet,
Felt in the blood, and felt along the heart;
And passing even into my purer mind,   30
With tranquil restoration: – feelings too
Of unremembered pleasure: such, perhaps,
As have no slight or trivial influence
On that best portion of a good man's life,
His little, nameless, unremembered, acts
Of kindness and of love. Nor less, I trust,
To them I may have owed another gift,
Of aspect more sublime; that blessed mood,

In which the burthen of the mystery,
In which the heavy and the weary weight   40
Of all this unintelligible world,
Is lightened: – that serene and blessed mood,
In which the affections gently lead us on, –
Until, the breath of this corporeal frame
And even the motion of our human blood
Almost suspended, we are laid asleep
In body, and become a living soul:
While with an eye made quiet by the power
Of harmony, and the deep power of joy,
We see into the life of things.   50
                                  If this
Be but a vain belief, yet, oh! how oft –
In darkness and amid the many shapes
Of joyless daylight; when the fretful stir
Unprofitable, and the fever of the world,
Have hung upon the beatings of my heart –
How oft, in spirit, have I turned to thee,
O sylvan Wye! thou wanderer thro' the woods,
How often has my spirit turned to thee!

And now, with gleams of half-extinguished thought,   60
With many recognitions dim and faint,
And somewhat of a sad perplexity,
The picture of the mind revives again:
While here I stand, not only with the sense
Of present pleasure, but with pleasing thoughts
That in this moment there is life and food
For future years. And so I dare to hope,
Though changed, no doubt, from what I was when first
I came among these hills; when like a roe
I bounded o'er the mountains, by the sides   70
Of the deep rivers, and the lonely streams,
Wherever nature led: more like a man
Flying from something that he dreads than one
Who sought the thing he loved. For nature then
(The coarser pleasures of my boyish days,
And their glad animal movements all gone by)
To me was all in all. – I cannot paint
What then I was. The sounding cataract
Haunted me like a passion: the tall rock,

The mountain and the deep and gloomy wood, 80
Their colours and their forms were then to me
An appetite; a feeling and a love,
That had no need of a remoter charm,
By thought supplied, nor any interest
Unborrowed from the eye. – That time is past,
And all its aching joys are now no more,
And all its dizzy raptures. Not for this
Faint I, nor mourn nor murmur; other gifts
Have followed; for such loss, I would believe,
Abundant recompense. For I have learned 90
To look on nature, not as in the hour
Of thoughtless youth; but hearing oftentimes
The still, sad music of humanity,
Nor harsh nor grating, though of ample power
To chasten and subdue. And I have felt
A presence that disturbs me with the joy
Of elevated thoughts; a sense sublime
Of something far more deeply interfused,
Whose dwelling is the light of setting suns,
And the round ocean and the living air, 100
And the blue sky, and in the mind of man:
A motion and a spirit, that impels
All thinking things, all objects of all thought,
And rolls through all things. Therefore am I still
A lover of the meadows and the woods,
And mountains; and of all that we behold
From this green earth; of all the mighty world
Of eye, and ear, – both what they half create,
And what perceive; well pleased to recognise
In nature and the language of the sense 110
The anchor of my purest thoughts, the nurse,
The guide, the guardian of my heart, and soul
Of all my moral being.
                              Nor perchance,
If I were not thus taught, should I the more
Suffer my genial spirits to decay:
For thou art with me here upon the banks
Of this fair river; thou my dearest Friend,
My dear, dear Friend; and in thy voice I catch
The language of my former heart, and read 120
My former pleasures in the shooting lights

Of thy wild eyes. Oh! yet a little while
May I behold in thee what I was once,
My dear, dear Sister! and this prayer I make,
Knowing that Nature never did betray
The heart that loved her; 'tis her privilege,
Through all the years of this our life, to lead
From joy to joy: for she can so inform
The mind that is within us, so impress
With quietness and beauty, and so feed   130
With lofty thoughts, that neither evil tongues,
Rash judgments, nor the sneers of selfish men,
Nor greetings where no kindness is, nor all
The dreary intercourse of daily life,
Shall e'er prevail against us, or disturb
Our cheerful faith, that all which we behold
Is full of blessings. Therefore let the moon
Shine on thee in thy solitary walk;
And let the misty mountain-winds be free
To blow against thee: and, in after years,   140
When these wild ecstasies shall be matured
Into a sober pleasure; when thy mind
Shall be a mansion for all lovely forms,
Thy memory be as a dwelling-place
For all sweet sounds and harmonies; oh! then,
If solitude, or fear, or pain, or grief,
Should be thy portion, with what healing thoughts
Of tender joy wilt thou remember me,
And these my exhortations! Nor, perchance –
If I should be where I no more can hear   150
Thy voice, nor catch from thy wild eyes these gleams
Of past existence – wilt thou then forget
That on the banks of this delightful stream
We stood together; and that I, so long
A worshipper of Nature, hither came
Unwearied in that service; rather say
With warmer love – oh! with far deeper zeal
Of holier love. Nor wilt thou then forget,
That after many wanderings, many years
Of absence, these steep woods and lofty cliffs,   160
And this green pastoral landscape, were to me
More dear, both for themselves and for thy sake!

William Wordsworth

Church Going

Once I am sure there's nothing going on
I step inside, letting the door thud shut.
Another church: matting, seats, and stone,
And little books; sprawlings of flowers, cut
For Sunday, brownish now; some brass and stuff
Up at the holy end; the small neat organ;
And a tense, musty, unignorable silence,
Brewed God knows how long. Hatless, I take off
My cycle-clips in awkward reverence.

Move forward, run my hand around the font.   10
From where I stand, the roof looks almost new –
Cleaned, or restored? Someone would know: I don't.
Mounting the lectern, I peruse a few
Hectoring large-scale verses, and pronounce
'Here endeth' much more loudly than I'd meant.
The echoes snigger briefly. Back at the door
I sign the book, donate an Irish sixpence,
Reflect the place was not worth stopping for.

Yet stop I did: in fact I often do,
And always end much at a loss like this,   20
Wondering what to look for; wondering, too,
When churches fall completely out of use
What we shall turn them into, if we shall keep
A few cathedrals chronically on show,
Their parchment, plate and pyx in locked cases,
And let the rest rent-free to rain and sheep.
Shall we avoid them as unlucky places?

Or, after dark, will dubious women come
To make their children touch a particular stone;
Pick simples for a cancer; or on some   30
Advised night see walking a dead one?
Power of some sort or other will go on
In games, in riddles, seemingly at random;
But superstition, like belief, must die,
And what remains when disbelief has gone?
Grass, weedy pavement, brambles, buttress, sky.

A shape less recognisable each week,
A purpose more obscure. I wonder who
Will be the last, the very last, to seek
This place for what it was; one of the crew   40
That tap and jot and know what rood-lofts were?
Some ruin-bibber, randy for antique,
Or Christmas-addict, counting on a whiff
Of gowns-and-bands and organ-pipes and myrrh?
Or will he be my representative.

Bored, uninformed, knowing the ghostly silt
Dispersed, yet tending to this cross of ground
Through suburb scrub because it held unspilt
So long and equably what since is found
Only in separation – marriage, and birth,   50
And death, and thoughts of these – for which was built
This special shell? For, though I've no idea
What this accoutred frowsty barn is worth,
It pleases me to stand in silence here;

A serious house on serious earth it is,
In whose blent air all our compulsions meet,
Are recognised, and robed as destinies.
And that much never can be obsolete,
Since someone will forever be surprising
A hunger in himself to be more serious,   60
And gravitating with it to this ground,
Which, he once heard, was proper to grow wise in,
If only that so many dead lie round.

Philip Larkin

Easter Morning – The African Intellectual

Ding dong bell
Pussy's in the well.

Another day....

Sleep leaves my opening eyes slowly
Unwillingly like a true lover.

But this day is different.
The lonely matin bells
Cut across the thin morning mist,
The glinting dew on the green grass,
The cool pink light before the heat of day,   10
The sudden punctual dawn of tropic skies,
Before the muezzin begins to cry,
Before the pagan drums begin to beat.

Easter morning.

But still for me
The great rock remains unrolled.
Within my wet dark tomb
Wounded peace remains embalmed,
The pricking thorns still yet my crown.

Easter morning.   20
Where are my ancestral spirits now?
I have forgotten for many harvests
To moisten the warm earth
With poured libations.
Where are you now, O Shango?
Two-headed, powerful
Man and woman, hermaphrodite
Holding your quivering thunderbolts
With quiet savage malice;
Brooding over your domain,   30
Africa, Cuba, Haiti, Brazil,
Slavery of mind is unabolished.
Always wanting to punish, never to love.

I have turned away from you
To One who stands
Watching His dying dispossessed Son
Shouting in Aramaic agony
Watching the white Picasso dove
Hovering above the Palestinian stream
Watching and waiting, sometimes   40
To punish, always to love.

Sleep confuses my tired mind
Still the bell rings
I must up and away.
I am a good Churchman, now.
Broadminded, which means past caring
Whether High or Low.
The priest may hold the chalice,
Or give it to me. It depends
On where he trained. I only mind   50
That he wipes the wet rim
Not to spread dental germs.
A tenth of my goods
I give to the poor
Through income tax

Easter morning.

Yet you Christ are always there.
You are the many-faceted crystal
Of our desires and hopes,
Behind the smoke-screen of incense,   60
Concealed in mumbled European tongues
Of worship and of praise.
In the thick dusty verbiage
Of centuries of committees
Of ecumenical councils.
You yet remain revealed
To those who seek you.
It is I, you say.
You remain in the sepulchre
Of my brown body.   70

Christ is risen, Christ is risen!

You were not dead.
It was just that we
Could not see clearly enough.
We can push out the rock from the inside.
You can come out now.
You see we want to share you
With our masters, because
You really are unique.

The great muddy river Niger,   80
Picks up the rising equatorial sun,
Changing itself by slow degrees
Into thick flowing molten gold.

Abioseh Nicol

In Westminster Abbey

Let me take this other glove off
    As the *vox humana* swells,
And the beauteous fields of Eden
    Bask beneath the Abbey bells.
Here, where England's statesmen lie,
Listen to a lady's cry.

Gracious Lord, oh bomb the Germans.
    Spare their women for Thy Sake,
And if that is not too easy
    We will pardon Thy Mistake.   10
But, gracious Lord, whate'er shall be,
Don't let anyone bomb me.

Keep our Empire undismembered
    Guide our Forces by Thy Hand,
Gallant blacks from far Jamaica,
    Honduras and Togoland;
Protect them Lord in all their fights,
And, even more, protect the whites.

Think of what our Nation stands for,
  Books from Boots' and country lanes,   20
Free speech, free passes, class distinction,
  Democracy and proper drains.
Lord, put beneath Thy special care
One-eighty-nine Cadogan Square.

Although dear Lord I am a sinner,
  I have done no major crime;
Now I'll come to Evening Service
  Whensoever I have the time.
So, Lord, reserve for me a crown,
And do not let my shares go down.   30

I will labour for Thy Kingdom,
  Help our lads to win the war,
Send white feathers to the cowards
  Join the Women's Army Corps,
Then wash the Steps around Thy Throne
In the Eternal Safety Zone.

Now I feel a little better,
  What a treat to hear Thy Word,
Where the bones of leading statesmen,
  Have so often been interr'd.   40
And now, dear Lord, I cannot wait
Because I have a luncheon date.

                    John Betjeman

Lyke-Wake Dirge

This ae nighte, this ae nighte,
  Every nighte and alle,
Fire and fleet and candle-lighte,
  And Christe receive thy saule.

When thou from hence away art past,
  Every nighte and alle,
To Whinny-muir thou com'st at last;
  And Christe receive thy saule.

If ever thou gavest hosen and shoon,
　Every nighte and alle.　　　　　　10
Sit thee down and put them on;
　And Christe receive thy saule.

If hosen and shoon thou ne'er gav'st nane
　Every nighte and alle,
The whinnes sall prick thee to the bare bane;
　And Christe receive thy saule.

From Whinny-Muir when thou art past,
　Every nighte and alle,
To Purgatory fire thou com'st at last;
　And Christe receive thy saule.　　　20

If ever thou gavest meat or drink,
　Every nighte and alle,
The fire sall never make thee shrink;
　And Christe receive thy saule.

If meat and drink you ne'er gav'st nane,
　Every nighte and alle,
The fire will burn thee to the bare bane
　And Christe receive thy saule.

This ae nighte, this ae nighte,
　Every nighte and alle,　　　　　　30
Fire and fleet and candle-lighte,
　And Christe receive thy saule.

Anonymous

London

I wander thro' each charter'd street,
Near where the charter'd Thames does flow,
And mark in every face I meet
Marks of weakness, marks of woe.

In every cry of every Man,
In every Infant's cry of fear,
In every voice, in every ban,
The mind-forg'd manacles I hear.

How the Chimney-sweeper's cry
Every black'ning Church appalls;
And the hapless soldier's sigh
Runs in blood down Palace walls.

But most thro' midnight streets I hear
How the youthful Harlot's curse
Blasts the new born Infant's tear,
And blights with plagues the Marriage hearse.

William Blake

Sonnet 116

Let me not to the marriage of true minds
Admit impediments, love is not love
Which alters when it alteration finds,
Or bends with the remover to remove.
O no, it is an ever-fixed mark
That looks on tempest and is never shaken;
It is the star to every wand'ring bark,
Whose worth's unknown, although his height be taken,
Love's not Time's fool, though rosy lips and cheeks
Within his bending sickle's compass come,
Love alters not with his brief hours and weeks,
But bears it out even to the edge of doom:
   If this be error and upon me proved,
   I never writ, nor no man ever loved.

William Shakespeare

Summer 1969

While the Constabulary covered the mob
Firing into the Falls, I was suffering
Only the bullying sun of Madrid.
Each afternoon, in the casserole heat
Of the flat, as I sweated my way through
The life of Joyce, stinks from the fishmarket
Rose like the reek off a flax-dam.
At night on the balcony, gules of wine,
A sense of children in their dark corners,
Old women in black shawls near open windows,   10
The air a canyon rivering in Spanish.
We talked our way home over starlit plains
Where patent leather of the Guardia Civil
Gleamed like fish-bellies in flax-poisoned waters.

'Go back,' one said, 'try to touch the people.'
Another conjured Lorca from his hill.
We sat through death counts and bullfight reports
On the television, celebrities
Arrived from where the real thing still happened.

I retreated to the cool of the Prado.   20
Goya's 'Shootings of the Third of May'
Covered a wall – the thrown-up arms
And spasm of the rebel, the helmeted
And knapsacked military, the efficient
Rake of the fusillade. In the next room
His nightmares, grafted to the palace wall –
Dark cyclones, hosting, breaking; Saturn
Jewelled in the blood of his own children,
Gigantic Chaos turning his brute hips
Over the world. Also, that holmgang   30
Where two berserks club each other to death
For honour's sake, greaved in a bog, and sinking.

He painted with his fists and elbows, flourished
The stained cape of his heart as history charged.

Seamus Heaney

EXAMPLES OF ESSAYS WRITTEN FOR EXAMINATIONS

Here are three examples from an English Literature examination of complete essays written on poetry by 16-year-old students. They are printed below, preceded by the question and followed by an examiner's mark scheme so that you can see the principles on which they were marked. The poems referred to in the question can be found printed in the appendix on pages 199–201.

Question: By close reference to any three of the following, illustrate the way Hopkins both describes vividly a particular scene in nature and also makes clear his thoughts about that scene: Inversnaid; Pied Beauty; Spring; Binsey Poplars.

(A) In Inversnaid Hopkins describes a Scottish burn. He uses the imagery of animals to produce the effect that the burn is a living creature. The colour is suggested by 'horse back brown' which changes to the image of a lion when it is 'roaring down'. Next the water becomes more gentle by the image of sheep in 'the fleece of its foam'.

The burn has power and also there is a feeling that it has purpose in where it is going, these two thoughts are inspired by the words 'rollrock highroad roaring down'.

In the next verse the water becomes quieter and gentle illustrated by the words 'windpuff and fawn-froth', the image of a fawn is used; a gentle and timid animal. It does not have such a sense of purpose now as it 'turns and twindles', then a great depression is hinted at as it 'rounds and rounds despair to drowning'. But this depression is not carried through to the third verse when the water emerges into open countryside. The nature here is quite thick as he talks of 'wiry heathpacks' and 'flitches of fern', the rhythm of 'degged with dew, dappled with dew are the groins of the braes that the brook treads through' gives the feeling that the water has to tread through the dense growth. A beautiful touch is added by the 'beadbonny ash that sits over the burn', it is as if the ash is the guardian of the burn.

In the last verse of 'Inversnaid' Hopkins seems to chant 'Let them be left, O let them be left'. He is afraid that the 'wildness and wet' will be destroyed by man. Although this is a rather happy poem about a beautiful Scottish burn at the end Hopkins is warning us not to let nature be destroyed.

In the first line of Spring Hopkins makes the statement that 'There is nothing so beautiful as Spring'. In the remainder of the first verse he qualifies this statement.

Hopkins describes the grass as 'long, lovely, lush' the rhythm suggests the feeling that they are growing.

The thrush's eggs are described as 'little low heavens' this beautiful piece of imagery suggests the eggs are perfect and also the beautiful light blue colour they are.

He feels cleansed by the thrush's song which 'rinses and wrings', there is also a feeling of perfection in the peartrees' 'glassy' leaves. They seem to paint the sky, and add to the harmony the sky rushes down to them.

In the second verse the philosopher comes out in Hopkins. He asks what is the meaning of all this beauty and says that it is as if they had returned to the garden of Eden. Suddenly panic seems to seize him, he says 'have, get, before it cloy', before it 'sours with sinning'. We must enjoy the nature before it is too late. This is also true with our lives, we all have our 'Maytime' when we are young and innocent. Hopkins is telling us to enjoy this time before it is ruined by sin.

Pied Beauty is rather like a hymn in poetic form. In the first line 'Glory be to God for dappled things', Hopkins seems to be telling us to enjoy nature. He thinks of all the things that are different colours, 'skies couple-coloured like a brinded cow' and the rose-moles 'All in a stipple'. The double 'p' in 'stipple' seems to pick out every dot singularly on its back.

His mind then turns to the cosyness of an autumn fire with 'hot fire coals' and 'chestnuts'. Then by pure inspiration he exclaims 'finches wings' and his excitement at this beauty is very effectively conveyed by his enthusiasm. He speaks of the landscape with its fields 'plotted and pieced'; it seems to have been designed by God.

In the second verse Hopkins points out that everything has its opposites, 'sweet and sour', 'swift and slow' but all the same everything is in harmony.

All things in nature are in a state of change, no one knows how this is done but it is an essential part of life. But Hopkins finds comfort in the fact that God never changes and therefore our love for him remains constant. Having proved to us the 'Pied beauty' of our world he ends the poem on a simple imperative, 'praise him'. He is satisfied that he has shown us the beauty of nature and that it is God we have to thank for it.

(B) Inversnaid is a very vivid poem. Hopkins involves sounds, descriptions and rhythms to portray the course of a Scottish river. The first verse is quite fast, like a stream, and the sounds are 'r's, 'c's and 'f's. For example: 'The rollrock highroad roaring down' – this depicts the tumbling of the stream over its rocky bed.

Another example is: 'In coop and in comb, the fleece of his foam'. The river is brown – 'horseback brown' shows an aspect of movement (in the horse) as well as colour, it also has 'fawn-froth'.

The next verse is slower and more sinister. It is pitchblack or 'rounds and rounds despair to drowning'. The sounds are longer and slow it down.

The third verse has Scottish sounding words such as 'braes', 'burns' and 'flitches', will tell us of its position.

The beauty of such a simple scene has been proved. One can see so much in it. So Hopkins appeals that the wildness and the wet be left if it is so beautiful.

'Long live the weeds and the wilderness yet.'

In Spring the first line shows how Hopkins is using long sounds to portray lushness i.e. Weeds in wheels, long, lovely and lush. It is noticeable that he finds beauty in weeds like in Inversnaid. He describes the thrush's eggs as 'little low heavens' which reveals part of the theme towards the end. The lambs depict innocence i.e. 'Mayday in girl and boy'. The purpose of the poem is to show the beauty and also appeal to us to appreciate it before 'spring' – a time of innocence – goes i.e. 'Have, get, before it cloy, before it cloud' and 'sour with sinning'.

The Binsley Poplars Hopkins regarded as his own were felled – the use of that word, a monosyllable that is repeated, emphasizes the finality of the act. His 'dear aspens' had a luxurious beauty no one appreciated i.e. 'Quenched in leaves the leaping sun'. Their removal is described with words usually used for torture such as 'hack' and 'rack' and his message is that 'where we mean to mend her we end her'. 'After-comers' will not be able to see the beauty that has been. The landscape has been 'unselved' – a Hopkins word meaning it has lost its identity.

(C) In Inversnaid Hopkins describes the beauty of a 'horseback-brown' stream rushing down a mountain side into a lake at the bottom:

'In coop and in comb the fleece of his foam
Flutes and low to the lake falls home.'

The water rushes into the lake and appears like a 'wind-puff bonnet' of foam before 'it rounds and rounds, despair to drowning'. The description of the scene is very beautiful as the water foams as it reaches the lake.
    In the sestet of this sonnet Hopkins says that the world would be a terrible place without such beautiful scenes.

'What would the world be, once bereft of wet and wildness?
Let them be left O let them be left.'

In the poem 'Spring' Hopkins describes all the beautiful spring activities and beauties of nature. The weeds that shoot 'long and lovely and lush' and the thrush's eggs 'look little low heavens' as they are dome shaped and produce new life. Also the lambs in the field have 'fair their fling'. In the sestet Hopkins goes on to say:

'What is all this juice and all this joy?
A strain of earth's sweet being in the beginning
In Eden garden.'

Hopkins asks why everyone is so happy and he wants all the children to be kept innocent and pure, like in 'Eden garden'. He does not want children to be 'soured with sinning'. Hopkins then prays to God and asks him to win over the minds of the children:

'Have, get, before it cloy
Before it cloud, Christ, Lord with sinning.'

71

In 'Binsey Poplars' Hopkins writes about a row of poplars who have been 'felled, all felled, are all felled'. It is a great shame as their function was to take the heat of the sun and give shade. The poplars stood 'in a fresh and following folded rank' and followed the curves of the riverside making the shadow of a sandal on the ground:

'That dandled a sandalled shadow that swam or sank,
On meadow and river, and wind-wandering, weed-winding bank.'

Hopkins says that the countryside is so delicate and 'even where we mean to mend her we end her' and people who come afterwards cannot see how beautiful it was.

Hopkins is greatly concerned with man's destruction of nature as 'strokes of havoc unselve' and it takes 'only ten or twelve' to destroy what has taken years to grow.

At the end Hopkins ponders on the situation:

'The sweet especial rural scene,
Rural scene, rural scene,
Sweet especial rural scene.'

This shows how the scene was dear to Hopkins and how the destruction lingers on in his mind.

What an examiner's mark scheme looks like

It is possible with a little shrewd reasoning to work out how the marks for an answer will probably be divided. For the question we have just looked at, it is clear that there will be an equal number of marks for each of the three poems covered by the candidate. Here is typical advice given to those marking the papers:

Mark 7 + 7 + 7 (Max. 20).

Since the thoughts are more obviously stated in some poems than in others, do not sub-divide the number of marks available for each poem. (That is, do not award, for instance, 4 for points on vivid description and 3 for points on clear thoughts.) But do not give more than 4 unless the candidate has made some attempt to separate thought from description. The question demands close reference so do not give more than 2 marks for a factual summary.

Here is how the three essays above were scored:

(A) Clearly an exceptionally good answer, which is easily worth a Grade A.
(B) Another good answer – this time just about worth a Grade A.
(C) A reasonably competent answer, which would comfortably earn a Grade C.

Go through each of the essays and see for yourself how far each candidate writes convincingly of the vivid description, and how far each candidate makes clear the thoughts of the poet.

Some comments on the examination essays

All of the above candidates answered the question well: (A) and (B) answered very well. Notice how useful their close knowledge of the text has been. Without a fairly detailed knowledge of a few poems it would not have been possible to answer the question satisfactorily.

This raises the question of the importance of knowing poetry 'by heart'. The above students show that their knowledge of the poems is more than parrot-learning. They produce appropriate material for the question asked, and they comment on the material, revealing an understanding of what they have learned.

Students often ask whether it is important to get the punctuation right in quotations, or the actual lines right, or the exact words. In the examples above you will see some errors made in all these aspects. Compare the versions of the students with the actual poems (printed in the appendix on page 199). Students will not 'lose marks' as long as they show a pretty accurate knowledge of the text; but the more accurate the knowledge the more convincing it is.

You might wonder about various other features of the above essays. For instance: the failure to use full stops accurately in (A); or the clumsy use of 'i.e.' in (B). Anything that strikes you as odd in these essays you should think about and discuss, since it is probably the kind of blemish which you should avoid yourself. The more prominent the blemish the greater is going to be its effect on any reader – including the examiner.

Further points on presentation

- Titles of poems should be distinguished in some way. An examiner will want to be able to tell at once whether you are referring to 'Binsey Poplars' the poems, or Binsey poplars the trees; and whether you mean 'Felix Randal' the poem or Felix Randal the man. In print, titles are usually indicated by being enclosed within quotation marks or printed in italics; in handwritten essays they ought to be underlined – freehand underlining will do if you do not have time to use a ruler.
- The incorrect spelling of an author's name is regarded as an indication of the student's lack of interest in an author. Make sure that you can spell the names of the few authors you study on your syllabus.
- The use of slang in your essays is an indication that, no matter what you might say about how effective a piece of writing is, you

73

really do not understand what kind of language is appropriate in a given context. If a character in a poem is courting a girl (or wooing her) it is not suitable to describe him as 'going with her'.

- Clichés can create similar bad impressions if you use them in your essays. They have the effect of making your writing look stale, stereotyped and mediocre instead of lively, personal and thoughtful.
- It is fine to say 'The poet says...' or 'The poet thinks...' but you should avoid the following expression, which is frequently used by thoughtless students: 'The poet is trying to say...' A moment's thought will tell you why.
- Remember that however much you know of a poem, always quote the shortest amount possible to support any given point you are making.

'Songs of other lands'

The Soldier

If I should die, think only this of me:
    That there's some corner of a foreign field
That is for ever England. There shall be
    In that rich earth a richer dust concealed;
A dust whom England bore, shaped, made aware,
    Gave, once, her flowers to love, her ways to roam,
A body of England's, breathing English air,
    Washed by the rivers, blest by suns of home.

And think, this heart, all evil shed away,
    A pulse in the eternal mind, no less
        Gives somewhere back the thoughts by England given;
Her sights and sounds; dreams happy as her day;
    And laughter, learnt of friends; and gentleness,
        In hearts at peace, under an English heaven.   *Rupert Brooke*

Anthem for Doomed Youth

What passing-bells for these who die as cattle?
    Only the monstrous anger of the guns.
    Only the stuttering rifles' rapid rattle
Can patter out their hasty orisons.
No mockeries now for them; no prayers nor bells,
    Nor any voice of mourning save the choirs, –
The shrill, demented choirs of wailing shells;
    And bugles calling for them from sad shires.

What candles may be held to speed them all?
    Not in the hands of boys, but in their eyes
Shall shine the holy glimmers of good-byes.
    The pallor of girls' brows shall be their pall;
Their flowers the tenderness of patient minds,
And each slow dusk a drawing-down of blinds.   *Wilfred Owen*

75

The Zulu Girl

When in the sun the hot red acres smoulder,
Down where the sweating gang its labour plies,
A girl flings down her hoe, and from her shoulder
Unslings her child tormented by the flies.

She takes him to a ring of shadow pooled
By thorn-trees: purples with the blood of ticks,
While her sharp nails, in slow caresses ruled,
Prowl through his hair with sharp electric clicks.

His sleepy mouth plugged by the heavy nipple,
Tugs like a puppy, grunting as he feeds: 10
Through his frail nerves her own deep languors ripple
Like a broad river sighing through its reeds.

Yet in that drowsy stream his flesh imbibes
An old unquenched unsmotherable heat –
The curbed ferocity of beaten tribes,
The sullen dignity of their defeat.

Her body looms above him like a hill
Within whose shade a village lies at rest.
Or the first cloud so terrible and still
That bears the coming harvest in its breast.   20

Roy Campbell

The Projectionist's Nightmare

This is the projectionist's nightmare:
A bird finds its way into the cinema,
finds the beam, flies down it,
smashes into a screen depicting a garden,
a sunset and two people being nice to each other.
Real blood, real intestines, slither down
the likeness of a tree.
'This is no good,' screams the audience,
'This is not what we came to see.'

Brian Patten

Death of a Naturalist

All year the flax-dam festered in the heart
Of the townland; green and heavy headed
Flax had rotted there, weighted down by huge sods.
Daily it sweltered in the punishing sun.
Bubbles gargled delicately, bluebottles
Wove a strong gauze of sound around the smell.
There were dragon-flies, spotted butterflies,
But best of all was the warm thick slobber
Of frogspawn that grew like clotted water
In the shade of the banks. Here, every spring   10
I would fill jampotfuls of the jellied
Specks to range on window-sills at home,
On shelves at school, and wait and watch until
The fattening dots burst into nimble-
Swimming tadpoles. Miss Walls would tell us how
The daddy frog was called a bullfrog
And how he croaked and how the mammy frog
Laid hundreds of little eggs and this was
Frogspawn. You could tell the weather by frogs too
For they were yellow in the sun and brown   20
In rain.

Then one hot day when fields were rank
With cowdung in the grass the angry frogs
Invaded the flax-dam; I ducked through hedges
To a coarse croaking that I had not heard
Before. The air was thick with a bass chorus.
Right down the dam gross-bellied frogs were cocked
On sods; their loose necks pulsed like sails. Some hopped:
The slap and plop were obscene threats. Some sat
Poised like mud grenades, their blunt heads farting.   30
I sickened, turned, and ran. The great slime kings
Were gathered there for vengeance and I knew
That if I dipped my hand the spawn would clutch it.

Seamus Heaney

Pike

Pike, three inches long, perfect
Pike in all parts, green tigering the gold.
Killers from the egg: the malevolent aged grin.
They dance on the surface among the flies.

Or move, stunned by their own grandeur,
Over a bed of emerald, silhouette
Of submarine delicacy and horror.
A hundred feet long in their world.

In ponds, under the heat-struck lily pads –
Gloom of their stillness: 10
Logged on last year's black leaves, watching upwards.
Or hung in an amber cavern of weeds

The jaws' hooked clamp and fangs
Not to be changed at this date;
A life subdued to its instrument;
The gills kneading quietly, and the pectorals.

Three we kept behind glass,
Jungled in weed: three inches, four,
And four and a half: fed fry to them –
Suddenly there were two. Finally one   20

With a sag belly and the grin it was born with.
And indeed they spare nobody.
Two, six pounds each, over two feet long,
High and dry and dead in the willow-herb –

One jammed past its gills down the other's gullet:
The outside eye stared: as a vice locks –
The same iron in this eye
Though its film shrank in death.

A pond, I fished, fifty yards across,
Whose lilies and muscular tench   30
Had outlasted every visible stone
Of the monastery that planted them –

Stilled legendary depth:
It was as deep as England. It held
Pike too immense to stir, so immense and old
That past nightfall I dared not cast

But silently cast and fished
With the hair frozen on my head
For what might move, for what eye might move.
The still splashes on the dark pond,   40

Owls hushing the floating woods
Frail on my ear against the dream
Darkness beneath night's darkness had freed,
That rose slowly towards me, watching.

Ted Hughes

Where's Agnes?

I

NAY, if I had come back so,
  And found her dead in her grave,
And if a friend I know
  Had said, 'Be strong, nor rave:
She lies there, dead below:

II

'I saw her, I who speak,
  White, stiff, the face one blank:
The blue shade came to her cheek
  Before they nailed the plank,
For she had been dead a week.'   10

III

Why, if he had spoken so,
  I might have believed the thing,
Although her look, although
  Her step, laugh, voice's ring
Lived in me still as they do.

IV

But dead that other way,
  Corrupted thus and lost?
That sort of worm in the clay?
  I cannot count the cost,
That I should rise and pay.   20

V

My Agnes false? such shame?
  She? Rather be it said
That the pure saint of her name
  Has stood there in her stead,
And tricked you to this blame.

VI

Her very gown, her cloak
  Fell chastely: no disguise,
But expression! while she broke
  With her clear grey morning-eyes
Full upon me and then spoke.   30

VII

She wore her hair away
  From her forehead, – like a cloud
Which a little wind in May
  Peels off finely: disallowed
Though bright enough to stay.

VIII

For the heavens must have the place
  To themselves, to use and shine in,
As her soul would have her face
  To press through upon mine, in
That orb of angel grace.   40

IX

Had she any fault at all,
  'Twas having none, I thought too –
There seemed a sort of thrall;
  As she felt her shadow ought to
Fall straight upon the wall.

X

Her sweetness strained the sense
  Of common life and duty;
And every day's expense
  Of moving in such beauty
Required, almost, defence.   50

XI

What good, I thought, is done
  By such sweet things, if any?
This world smells ill i' the sun
  Though the garden-flowers are many, –
She is only one.

XII

Can a voice so low and soft
  Take open actual part
With Right, – maintain aloft
  Pure truth in life or art,
Vexed always, wounded oft? –   60

XIII

She fit, with that fair pose
  Which melts from curve to curve,
To stand, run, work with those
  Who wrestle and deserve,
And speak plain without glose?

XIV

But I turned round on my fear
  Defiant, disagreeing –
What if God has set her here
  Less for action than for Being? –
For the eye and for the ear.   70

XV

Just to show what beauty may,
  Just to prove what music can, –
And then to die away
  From the presence of a man,
Who shall learn, henceforth, to pray?

XVI

As a door, left half ajar
  In heaven, would make him think
How heavenly-different are
  Things glanced at through the chink,
Till he pined from near to far.   80

XVII

That door could lead to hell?
  That shining merely meant
Damnation? What! She fell
  Like a woman, who was sent
Like an angel, by a spell?

XVIII

She, who scarcely trod the earth,
  Turned mere dirt? My Agnes, – mine!
Called so! felt of too much worth
  To be used so! too divine
To be breathed near, and so forth!   90

XIX

Why, I dared not name a sin
  In her presence: I went round,
Clipped its name and shut it in
  Some mysterious crystal sound, –
Changed the dagger for the pin.

XX

Now you name herself *that word?*
  O my Agnes! O my saint!
Then the great joys of the Lord
  Do not last? Then all this paint
Runs off nature? leaves a board?   100

XXI

Who's dead here? No, not she:
  Rather I! or whence this damp
Cold corruption's misery?
  While my very mourners stamp
Closer in the clods on me.

XXII

And my mouth is full of dust
  Till I cannot speak and curse –
Speak and damn him...'Blame's unjust'?
  Sin blots out the universe,
All because she would and must?   110

XXIII

She, my white rose, dropping off
  The high rose-tree branch! and not
That the night-wind blew too rough,
  Or the noon-sun burnt too hot,
But, that being a rose – 'twas enough!

XXIV

Then henceforth, may earth grow trees!
  No more roses! – hard straight lines
To score lies out! none of these
  Fluctuant curves! but firs and pines,
Poplars, cedars, cypresses!   120

Elizabeth Barrett Browning

A Hard Frost

A frost came in the night and stole my world
And left this changeling for it – a precocious
Image of spring, too brilliant to be true:
White lilac on the windowpane, each grass-blade
Furred like a catkin, maydrift loading the hedge.
The elms behind the house are elms no longer
But blossomers in crystal, stems of the mist
That hangs yet in the valley below, amorphous
As the blind tissue whence creation formed.

The sun looks out, and the fields blaze with diamonds.
Mockery spring, to lend this bridal gear
For a few hours to a raw country maid,
Then leave her all disconsolate with old fairings
Of aconite and snowdrop! No, not here
Amid this flounce and filigree of death
Is the real transformation scene in progress
But deep below where frost
Worrying the stiff clods unclenches their
Grip on the seed and lets our future breathe.

C. Day Lewis

A Whiter Shade of Pale

We skipped the light fandango
And turned cartwheels cross the floor.
I was feeling kind of seasick
But the crowd called out for more.
The room was humming harder
As the ceiling flew away
When we called out for another drink
The waiter brought a tray
And so it was that later
As the miller told his tale   10
That her face at first just ghostly
Turned a whiter shade of pale.

She said 'There is no reason,
And the truth is plain to see,'
But I wandered through my playing cards
And would not let her be
One of sixteen vestal virgins
Who were leaving for the coast
And although my eyes were open
They might just have well been closed.   20
And so it was that later
As the miller told his tale
That her face at first just ghostly
Turned a whiter shade of pale.

Keith Reid & Gary Brooker

They flee from me, that sometime did me seek

They flee from me, that sometime did me seek
With naked foot, stalking in my chamber.
I have seen them gentle, tame, and meek,
That now are wild, and do not remember
That sometime they put themselves in danger
To take bread at my hand; and now they range
Busily seeking with a continual change.

Thanked be fortune it hath been otherwise
Twenty times better; but once, in special,
In thin array, after a pleasant guise,   10
When her loose gown from her shoulders did fall,
And she me caught in her arms long and small,
Therewith all sweetly did me kiss
And softly said, 'Dear heart, now like you this?'

It was no dream; I lay broad waking:
But all is turned, thorough my gentleness,
Into a strange fashion of forsaking;
And I have leave to go of her goodness,
And she also to use newfangleness.
But since that I so kindly am served,   20
I would fain know what she hath deserved.

Sir Thomas Wyatt

A Poison Tree

I was angry with my friend:
I told my wrath, my wrath did end.
I was angry with my foe:
I told it not, my wrath did grow.

And I water'd it in fears,
Night & morning with my tears;
And I sunned it with smiles,
And with soft deceitful wiles.

And it grew both day and night,
Till it bore an apple bright;
And my foe beheld it shine,
And he knew that it was mine,

And into my garden stole
When the night had veil'd the pole:
In the morning glad I see
My foe outstretch'd beneath the tree.

William Blake

La Belle Dame Sans Merci

I

O, what can ail thee, knight-at-arms,
    Alone and palely loitering?
The sedge has wither'd from the lake,
    And no birds sing.

II

O, what can ail thee, knight-at-arms,
    So haggard and so woe-begone?
The squirrel's granary is full,
    And the harvest's done.

III

I see a lilly on thy brow,
    With anguish moist and fever dew;   10
And on thy cheeks a fading rose
    Fast withereth too.

IV

I met a lady in the meads,
    Full beautiful – a faery's child,
Her hair was long, her foot was light,
    And her eyes were wild.

V

I made a garland for her head,
    And bracelets too, and fragrant zone;
She look'd at me as she did love,
    And made sweet moan.   20

VI

I set her on my pacing steed,
    And nothing else saw all day long;
For sidelong would she bend, and sing
    A faery's song.

VII

She found me roots of relish sweet,
   And honey wild, and manna dew,
And sure in language strange she said –
   'I love thee true'.

VIII

She took me to her elfin grot,
   And there she wept and sigh'd full sore,   30
And there I shut her wild wild eyes
   With kisses four.

IX

And there she lulled me asleep
   And there I dream'd – Ah! woe betide!
The latest dream I ever dream'd
   On the cold hill side.

X

I saw pale kings and princes too,
   Pale warriors, death-pale were they all;
They cried – 'La Belle Dame sans Merci
   Hath thee in thrall!'   40

XI

I saw their starved lips in the gloam,
   With horrid warning gaped wide,
And I awoke and found me here,
   On the cold hill's side.

XII

And this is why I sojourn here
   Alone and palely loitering,
Though the sedge has wither'd from the lake,
   And no birds sing.

John Keats

Kubla Khan

In Xanadu did Kubla Khan
A stately pleasure-dome decree:
Where Alph, the sacred river, ran
Through caverns measureless to man
   Down to a sunless sea.
So twice five miles of fertile ground
With walls and towers were girdled round:
And there were gardens bright with sinuous rills,
Where blossomed many an incense-bearing tree;
And here were forests ancient as the hills,   10
Enfolding sunny spots of greenery.

But oh! that deep romantic chasm which slanted
Down the green hill athwart a cedarn cover!
A savage place! as holy and enchanted
As e'er beneath a waning moon was haunted
By woman wailing for her demon-lover!
And from this chasm, with ceaseless turmoil seething,
As if this earth in fast thick pants were breathing,
A mighty fountain momently was forced:
Amid whose swift half-intermitted burst   20
Huge fragments vaulted like rebounding hail,
Or chaffy grain beneath the thresher's flail:
And 'mid these dancing rocks at once and ever
It flung up momently the sacred river.
Five miles meandering with a mazy motion
Through wood and dale the sacred river ran,
Then reached the caverns measureless to man,
And sank in tumult to a lifeless ocean:
And 'mid this tumult Kubla heard from far
Ancestral voices prophesying war!   30

   The shadow of the dome of pleasure
   Floated midway on the waves;
   Where was heard the mingled measure
   From the fountain and the caves.
It was a miracle of rare device,
A sunny pleasure-dome with caves of ice!

A damsel with a dulcimer
In a vision once I saw:
It was an Abyssinian maid,
And on her dulcimer she play'd,   40
Singing of Mount Abora.
Could I revive within me
Her symphony and song,
To such a deep delight 'twould win me,
That with music loud and long,
I would build that dome in air,
That sunny dome! those caves of ice!
And all who heard should see them there,
And all should cry, Beware! Beware!
His flashing eyes, his floating hair!   50
Weave a circle round him thrice,
And close your eyes with holy dread:
For he on honey-dew hath fed,
And drunk the milk of Paradise.

S. T. Coleridge

The Demon Lover

1
'O where have you been, my dear, dear love,
    This long seven years and more?'
'O I'm come to seek my former vows
    Ye granted me before.'

2
'O hold your tongue of your former vows,
    For they will breed sad strife;
O hold your tongue of your former vows,
    For I am become a wife.'

3
He turned him right and round about,
    And the tear blinded his ee;   10
'I would never have trodden on Irish ground,
    If it had not been for thee.

4

'I might have had a king's daughtér
  Far, far beyond the sea;
I might have had a king's daughtér,
  Were it not for love of thee.'

5

'If ye might have had a king's daughtér,
  Yourself ye had to blame;
Ye might have taken the king's daughtér,
  For ye kenned that I was nane.   20

6

'If I were to leave my husband dear,
  And my two babes also,
O what have you to take me to,
  If with you I should go?'

7

'I have seven ships upon the sea,
  The eighth brought me to land;
With four and twenty bold mariners.
  And music on every hand.'

8

She has taken up her two little babes,
  Kissed them both cheek and chin;   30
'O fare ye well, my own two babes,
  For I'll never see you again.'

9

She set her foot upon the ship,
  No mariners could she behold;
But the sails were of the taffety,
  And the masts of the beaten gold.

10

She had not sailed a league, a league,
  A league but barely three,
When dismal grew his countenance,
  And drumlie¹ grew his ee.   40

11

They had not sailed a league, a league,
  A league but barely three,
Until she espied his cloven foot,
  And she wept right bitterly.

12

'O hold your tongue of your weeping,' says he
  'Of your weeping now let me be;
I will show you how the lilies grow
  On the banks of Italy.'

13

'O what hills are they, those pleasant hills,
  That the sun shines sweetly on?'   50
'O those are the hills of Heaven,' he said,
  'Where you shall never wone².'

14

'O whaten a mountain is that,' she said,
  'So dreary with frost and snow?'
'O that is the mountain of Hell,' he cried,
  'Where you and I must go.'

15

He struck the top-mast with his hand,
  The fore-mast with his knee;
And he brake that gallant ship in twain,
  And sank her in the sea.   60

Anonymous

¹ gloomy   ² live

Leda and the Swan

A sudden blow: the great wings beating still
Above the staggering girl, her thighs caressed
By the dark webs, her nape caught in his bill,
He holds her helpless breast upon his breast.

How can those terrified vague fingers push
The feathered glory from her loosening thighs?
And how can body, laid in that white rush,
But feel the strange heart beating where it lies?

A shudder in the loins engenders there
The broken wall, the burning roof and tower
And Agamemnon dead.
                 Being so caught up,
So mastered by the brute blood of the air,
Did she put on his knowledge with his power
Before the indifferent beak could let her drop?

                        W. B. Yeats

The Shipwreck

Glee! the great storm is over!
Four have recovered the land;
Forty gone down together
Into the boiling sand.

Ring, for the scant salvation!
Toll, for the bonnie souls, –
Neighbor and friend and bridegroom,
Spinning upon the shoals!

How they will tell the shipwreck
When winter shakes the door,
Till the children ask, 'But the forty?
Did they come back no more?'

Then a silence suffuses the story,
And a softness the teller's eye;
And the children no further question,
And only the waves reply.   *Emily Dickinson*

We Have Come Home

We have come home
From the bloodless wars
With sunken hearts
Our boots full of pride –
From the true massacre of the soul
When we have asked
'What does it cost
To be loved and left alone'.

We have come home
Bringing the pledge   1●
Which is written in rainbow colours
Across the sky – for burial
But it is not the time
To lay wreaths
For yesterday's crimes.
Night threatens
Time dissolves
And there is no acquaintance
With tomorrow.

The gurgling drums   2●
Echo the stars
The forest howls
And between the trees
The dark sun appears.

We have come home
When the dawn falters
Singing songs of other lands
The death march
Violating our ears
Knowing all our loves and tears   3●
Determined by the spinning coin.

We have come home
To the green foothills
To drink from the cup
Of warm and mellow birdsong
To the hot beaches
Where the boats go out to sea
Threshing the ocean's harvest
And the hovering, plunging
Gliding gulls shower kisses on the waves.   40

We have come home
Where through the lightning flash
And thundering rain
The famine the drought,
The sudden spirit
Lingers on the road
Supporting the tortured remnants of the flesh
That spirit which asks no favour of the world
But to have dignity.

Lenrie Peters

On His Blindness

When I consider how my light is spent,
  Ere half my days, in this dark world and wide,
  And that one Talent which is death to hide,
  Lodg'd with me useless, though my Soul more bent
To serve therewith my Maker, and present
  My true account, least he returning chide,
  Doth God exact day-labour, light deny'd,
  I fondly ask; But patience to prevent
That murmur, soon replies, God doth not need
  Either man's work or his own gifts, who best
  Bear his milde yoak, they serve him best, his State
Is Kingly. Thousands at his bidding speed
  And post o're Land and Ocean without rest:
  They also serve who only stand and waite.

John Milton

Fern Hill

Now as I was young and easy under the apple boughs
About the lilting house and happy as the grass was green,
   The night above the dingle starry,
     Time let me hail and climb
   Golden in the heydays of his eyes,
And honoured among wagons I was prince of the apple towns
And once below a time I lordly had the trees and leaves
   Trail with daisies and barley
   Down the rivers of the windfall light.

And as I was green and carefree, famous among the barns 10
About the happy yard and singing as the farm was home,
   In the sun that is young once only,
     Time let me play and be
   Golden in the mercy of his means,
And green and golden I was huntsman and herdsman, the
     calves
Sang to my horn, the foxes on the hills barked clear and cold,
   And the sabbath rang slowly
   In the pebbles of the holy streams.

All the sun long it was running, it was lovely, the hay
Fields high as the house, the tunes from the chimneys, it was air 20
   And playing, lovely and watery
     And fire green as grass.
   And nightly under the simple stars
As I rode to sleep the owls were bearing the farm away,
All the moon long I heard, blessed among stables, the nightjars
   Flying with the ricks, and the horses
     Flashing into the dark.

And then to awake, and the farm, like a wanderer white
With the dew, come back, the cock on his shoulder: it was all
   Shining, it was Adam and maiden, 30
     The sky gathered again
   And the sun grew round that very day.
So it must have been after the birth of the simple light
In the first, spinning place, the spellbound horses walking warm
   Out of the whinnying green stable
     On to the fields of praise.

And honoured among foxes and pheasants by the gay house
Under the new made clouds and happy as the heart was long,
   In the sun born over and over,
     I ran my heedless ways,   40
   My wishes raced through the house high hay
And nothing I cared, at my sky blue trades, that time allows
In all his tuneful turning so few and such morning songs
   Before the children green and golden
     Follow him out of grace,

Nothing I cared, in the lamb white days, that time would take
     me
Up to the swallow thronged loft by the shadow of my hand,
   In the moon that is always rising,
     Nor that riding to sleep
   I should hear him fly with the high fields   50
And wake to the farm forever fled from the childless land.
Oh as I was young and easy in the mercy of his means,
     Time held me green and dying
    Though I sang in my chains like the sea.

Dylan Thomas

Snow

The room was suddenly rich and the great bay-window was
Spawning snow and pink roses against it
Soundlessly collateral and incompatible:
World is suddener than we fancy it.

World is crazier and more of it than we think,
Incorrigibly plural. I peel and portion
A tangerine and spit the pips and feel
The drunkenness of things being various.

And the fire flames with a bubbling sound for world
Is more spiteful and gay than one supposes –
On the tongue on the eyes on the ears in the palms of one's
   hands –
There is more than glass between the snow and the huge roses.

Louis MacNeice

Snakecharmer

As the gods began one world, and man another,
So the snakecharmer begins a snaky sphere
With moon-eye, mouth-pipe. He pipes. Pipes green. Pipes water.

Pipes water green until green waters waver
With reedy lengths and necks and undulatings.
And as his notes twine green, the green river

Shapes its images around his songs.
He pipes a place to stand on, but no rocks,
No floor: a wave of flickering grass tongues

Supports his foot. He pipes a world of snakes,   10
Of sways and coilings, from the snake-rooted bottom
Of his mind. And now nothing but snakes

Is visible. The snake-scales have become
Leaf, become eyelid; snake-bodies, bough, breast
Of tree and human. And he within this snakedom

Rules the writhings which make manifest
His snakehood and his might with pliant tunes
From his thin pipe. Out of this green nest

As out of Eden's navel twist the lines
Of snaky generations: let there be snakes!   20
And snakes there were, are, will be – till yawns

Consume this piper and he tires of music
And pipes the world back to the simple fabric
Of snake-warp, snake-weft. Pipes the cloth of snakes

To a melting of green waters, till no snake
Shows its head, and those green waters back to
Water, to green, to nothing like a snake.
Puts up his pipe, and lids his moony eye.

Sylvia Plath

The Going

Why did you give no hint that night
That quickly after the morrow's dawn,
And calmly, as if indifferent quite,
You would close your term here, up and be gone
    Where I could not follow
    With wing of swallow
To gain one glimpse of you ever anon!

Never to bid good-bye,
    Or lip me the softest call,
Or utter a wish for a word, while I   10
Saw morning harden upon the wall,
    Unmoved, unknowing
    That your great going
Had place that moment, and altered all.

Why do you make me leave the house
And think for a breath it is you I see
At the end of the alley of bending boughs
Where so often at dusk you used to be;
    Till in darkening dankness
    The yawning blankness   20
Of the perspective sickens me!

    You were she who abode
    By those red-veined rocks far West,
You were the swan-necked one who rode
Along the beetling Beeny Crest,
    And, reining nigh me,
    Would muse and eye me,
While Life unrolled us its very best.

Why, then, latterly did we not speak,
Did we not think of those days long dead,   30
And ere your vanishing strive to seek
That time's renewal? We might have said,
    'In this bright spring weather
    We'll visit together
Those places that once we visited.'

Well, well! All's past amend,
Unchangeable. It must go.
I seem but a dead man held on end
To sink down soon...O you could not know
    That such swift fleeing   40
    No soul foreseeing –
Not even I – would undo me so!

          Thomas Hardy

BUILDING AND ANNOTATING AN ANTHOLOGY

Writing essays about poems is not the only way to demonstrate a positive response to poetry. To make a collection of poems you enjoy is in itself a reflection of your taste and interest in poetry; it is an activity which poetry-lovers have always indulged in. Of course, people who make up their own anthologies are usually under no compulsion to do so. They have nothing to prove to anybody. Students approaching examinations in English do have to prove something to the examiner. They have to prove that the poems they have selected represent more than the slavish chore of mere copying out.

The easiest way to do this is to write notes to accompany the poems – notes which indicate why you like the poem or what you find interesting in it. This is exactly what people do when they talk about poetry (or anything else they like, for that matter). This is also what teachers do when they teach poetry. They do not produce the spoken equivalent of essays, which would be carefully argued and cogent lectures; they draw attention to different parts of the poem, explain things which they think might cause difficulty in understanding, ask questions, consider possibilities.

Teachers are successful when they convey an enthusiasm for the poem to their students. Teachers do not do this simply by telling the class that they like the poem. Enthusiasm is conveyed by the way teachers highlight, through talking about them, the features of the poem which interest them. Students often come to like poems their teachers discuss with them. Teachers are initiators. But students ought to reach the stage where they make their own judgments, select their own poems, and are able to persuade other readers to enjoy them.

Read, for example, the following poem:

The Eagle

He clasps the crag with crooked hands;
Close to the sun in lonely lands,
Ringed with the azure world he stands.

The wrinkled world beneath him crawls;
He watches from his mountain walls,
And like a thunderbolt he falls.   *Alfred, Lord Tennyson*

100

Here are annotations of the poem by three different students. Which one makes you feel most interest in the poem?

(A) Azure means the blue of the sky. In the first line the poet uses alliteration, beginning three words with 'c'. There is a very clear image created of the eagle's loneliness on the rock as it waits to swoop on its prey. Each verse rhymes in every line.

(B) The eagle stands on his crag looking like a monarch in his tower. He is 'ringed with the azure world' as if he is in a portrait frame. There is also a suggestion that he is the centre of his world, which is emphasized by 'his mountain walls', as if the mountain is his castle. The hard 'c' sounds in the first line draw attention to his claws and their cruelty. At the end of the poem this cruelty is brought out in the terror of the eagle's plunge towards his prey – like a thunderbolt.

(C) It seems odd to call an eagle's claws crooked hands – it suggests something sinister about him. Why is he described as 'close to the sun'? Maybe it makes him seem more powerful. Or maybe it is to show how high up above the sea he is. 'Ringed' – is this because the sun forms a ring of light around him? I like 'wrinkled' to describe the movement of the sea far below him. 'He watches' shows how still he is in his concentration, until he sees his prey beneath him and descends with violence. This probably explains the sinister effect in the first line.

(A) is very weak because the notes do not give us much insight into the poem. Nor has the student allowed himself much opportunity to indicate a personal response to the poem. He says that the poet uses alliteration of 'c' in the first line, but does not say what this achieves in the poem. Even without using the technical term 'alliteration', (B) is able to make clear the effect of alliteration. This is a great improvement on (A).

(C) is far less confident in the notes, but shows a thoughtful and sensitive approach. What is important is that the questions in the notes highlight the poem's interesting features, or at least those features which interest (C). It is a personal response and it is interesting to the reader. There is certainly nothing wrong in this approach, which is like thinking aloud. Both (B) and (C) are good examples of students who display an intelligent sensitivity to the poem through their annotations.

How long should the poems be?

There is neither an upper nor a lower limit, though clearly a collection of long poems would be very time-consuming, especially if they all have to be copied out by hand. You might well find that the writing out of several long poems did not leave you enough time to annotate them thoroughly. On the other hand an anthology full of very short poems might not offer you enough scope to make many points in response. And it is just possible that a collection of very short poems might be regarded as a lack of enthusiasm; this would depend on the extent of the annotations.

Here are three more examples of students' annotations of poems. In the light of the comments on the earlier examples discuss or write down what you consider the strengths and weaknesses of each.

Spanish Harlem

There is a rose in Spanish Harlem,
A red rose up in Spanish Harlem.
It is a special one;
It's never seen the sun,
It only comes out when the moon is on the run
And all the stars are gleaming.
It's growing in the street
Right up through the concrete
But soft and sweet and dreaming.

There is a rose in Spanish Harlem,
A red rose up in Spanish Harlem
With eyes as black as coal
That look down in my soul
And start a fire there and then I lose control.
I have to beg your pardon,
I'm going to pick that rose
And watch her as she grows
In my garden.

Ben E. King

(A) This poem is the lyric of a pop song by a singer named Ben E. King, though I do not think he wrote the song. It is about a girl that the singer has fallen in love with who is very beautiful. He says he is going to pick that rose, which means he is going to marry her and take her away from Harlem to live with him. He will then be able to look at her all the time.

(B) Ben E. King's song is difficult to make sense of. What does he mean by 'when the moon is on the run'?

How can a rose grow up through the concrete – unless he means a gap in the paving stones. He says the rose is red, but that it has eyes as black as coal. The rose is meant to be a beautiful girl, but I don't see how she can be red in that case. If it is a girl then she could not grow up through the concrete. The song has to have the music to it to be really appreciated. It sounds really good then, especially the last line of each verse. That's why I chose it.

(C) Harlem is the part of New York which has a very large black population. It is also a slum. The poet has noticed a very beautiful woman there, who is as beautiful as a red rose. He is surprised that anyone so beautiful can live in a district like Harlem. She is like an exotic plant which is carefully cultivated in the city, which has the power to convert the slums, as suggested by the idea of a flower bursting up through the concrete. But she is not aggressive, only 'soft and sweet and dreaming'.

The poet obviously sees her in the evenings, when the stars make his courtship seem very romantic. I think he begs the pardon of everybody because he is so infatuated with the girl that he is going to take her away to live with him. He will be taking the only beautiful thing from the slum, which is its environment, to be placed in his house. The idea is ambiguous because the girl was clearly kept out of sight during the day time in Harlem, or at least she kept her beauty hidden during the day. Harlem might be seen therefore as an alien environment for her.

Finding poems for your own anthology

1. Author, theme or topic?

Through reading the poems in this anthology you will be introduced to a wide range of poetic styles and historical periods. From here you can go to other poems by an author whose work you have enjoyed. Or you can look for other poems on subjects or themes which interest you. It is sometimes easier to find a book of poems by a given author than a book of poems on a given theme. Besides, every poem makes its own unique appeal by the writer's sensitive handling of the language. It is more likely, therefore, that a writer whose handling of the language makes an impact on you with one poem will do so with another, than that another writer will make a similar impact merely by writing on the same subject. On the other hand, some themes attract a good deal of good writing. For instance, students often become fascinated by the poetry of the First World War, finding in the various poets of the period a range of different attitudes which are expressed with equal vigour.

2. A few at a time

Because the language of poetry is so compact, and because the sequences of thought sometimes emerge rather subtly, poems often need three or four readings before they can be properly appreciated. It is better to read carefully a few poems at a time than to skim through large numbers of them. To speed through a poem is not really to give it a fair chance of making an impression on you.

3. Sharing ideas

If your knowledge of poetry is rather limited, then seek advice from your teacher. Your teacher will not only have read many more poems than you, but will also know the best way you can get hold of poems by authors you like.

Discuss with your friends their choices. Their enthusiasm for poems they really enjoy might be enough to make you enjoy them too. When building an anthology it can be fun to compare your own with your friends' as you progress.

Sometimes it is a good idea to read a favourite poem out to the class, or to a small group within the class. If you do not like actually reading it aloud yourself, then ask your teacher to do so. Hearing a poem read aloud can often make it more appealing than simply reading it on the page.

'This changeful life'

Mending Wall

Something there is that doesn't love a wall,
That sends the frozen-ground-swell under it,
And spills the upper boulders in the sun;
And makes gaps even two can pass abreast.
The work of hunters is another thing:
I have come after them and made repair
Where they have left not one stone on a stone,
But they would have the rabbit out of hiding,
To please the yelping dogs. The gaps I mean,
No one has seen them made or heard them made,   10
But at spring mending-time we find them there.
I let my neighbour know beyond the hill;
And on a day we meet to walk the line
And set the wall between us once again.
We keep the wall between us as we go.
To each the boulders that have fallen to each.
And some are loaves and some so nearly balls
We have to use a spell to make them balance:
'Stay where you are until our backs are turned!'
We wear our fingers rough with handling them.   20
Oh, just another kind of outdoor game,
One on a side. It comes to little more:
There where it is we do not need the wall:
He is all pine and I am apple orchard.
My apple trees will never get across
And eat the cones under his pines, I tell him.
He only says, 'Good fences make good neighbours'.
Spring is the mischief in me, and I wonder
If I could put a notion in his head:
'Why do they make good neighbours? Isn't it   30
Where there are cows? But here there are no cows.
Before I built a wall I'd ask to know
What I was walling in or walling out,
And to whom I was like to give offence.

Something there is that doesn't love a wall,
That wants it down.' I could say 'Elves' to him,
But its not elves exactly, and I'd rather
He said it for himself. I see him there
Bringing a stone grasped firmly by the top
In each hand, like an old-stone savage armed.   40
He moves in darkness as it seems to me,
Not of woods only and the shade of trees.
He will not go behind his father's saying,
And he likes having thought of it so well
He says again, 'Good fences make good neighbours'.

Robert Frost

South Cumberland, 10th May 1943

The fat flakes fall
In parachute invasion from the yellow sky.
The streets are quiet and surprised; the snow
Clutters the roofs with a wet crust, but no
Dry harbour is found on soil or wall.

In the town
The fledgling sparrows are puzzled and take fright;
The weedy hair of the slagbank in an hour turns white.
Flakes fill the tulips in backyard plots;
The chimneys snow upward and the snow smokes down.   10

Beyond the fells
Dawn lumbers up, and the peaks are white through the mist.
The young bracken is buttoned with snow, the knobs
Of crabapple trees are in bloom again, and blobs
Hang on the nettles like Canterbury bells.

This job is mine
And everyone's: to force our blood into the bitter day.
The hawthorn scorched and blasted by the flames of the wind
On the sheltered side greens out a dogged spray –
And this is our example, our duty and our sign.   20

Norman Nicholson

Follower

My father worked with a horse-plough,
His shoulders globed like a full sail strung
Between the shafts and the furrow.
The horses strained at his clicking tongue.

An expert. He would set the wing
And fit the bright steel-pointed sock.
The sod rolled over without breaking.
At the headrig, with a single pluck

Of reins, the sweating team turned round
And back into the land. His eye   10
Narrowed and angled at the ground,
Mapping the furrow exactly.

I stumbled in his hob-nailed wake,
Fell sometimes on the polished sod;
Sometimes he rode me on his back
Dipping and rising to his plod.

I wanted to grow up and plough,
To close one eye, stiffen my arm.
All I ever did was follow
In his broad shadow round the farm.   20

I was a nuisance, tripping, falling,
Yapping always. But today
It is my father who keeps stumbling
Behind me, and will not go away.

Seamus Heaney

Our History
to pre-colonial Africa

And the waves arrived
Swimming in like hump-backed divers
With their finds from far-away seas.

Their lustre gave the illusion of pearls
As shorewards they shoved up mighty canoes
And looked like the carcass of drifting whales.

And our sight misled us
When the sun's glint on the spear's blade
Passed for lightning
And the gun-fire of conquest
The thunderbolt that razed the forest.

So did our days change their garb
From hides of leopard skin
To prints of false lions
That fall in tatters
Like the wings of whipped butterflies.

Mbella Sonne Dipoko

Ulysses

It little profits that an idle king,
By this still hearth, among these barren crags,
Match'd with an aged wife, I mete and dole
Unequal laws unto a savage race,
That hoard, and sleep, and feed, and know not me.
I cannot rest from travel: I will drink
Life to the lees: all times I have enjoy'd
Greatly, have suffer'd greatly, both with those
That loved me, and alone; on shore, and when
Thro' scudding drifts the rainy Hyades   10
Vext the dim sea: I am become a name;
For always roaming with a hungry heart
Much have I seen and known; cities of men
And manners, climates, councils, governments,
Myself not least, but honour'd of them all;
And drunk delight of battle with my peers,
Far on the ringing plains of windy Troy.
I am a part of all that I have met;
Yet all experience is an arch wherethro'
Gleams that untravell'd world, whose margin fades   20

For ever and for ever when I move.
How dull it is to pause, to make an end,
To rust unburnish'd, not to shine in use!
As tho' to breathe were life. Life piled on life
Were all too little, and of one to me
Little remains: but every hour is saved
From that eternal silence, something more,
A bringer of new things; and vile it were
For some three suns to store and hoard myself,
And this gray spirit yearning in desire   30
To follow knowledge like a sinking star,
Beyond the utmost bound of human thought.
    This is my son, mine own Telemachus,
To whom I leave the sceptre and the isle –
Well-loved of me, discerning to fulfil
This labour, by slow prudence to make mild
A rugged people, and thro' soft degrees
Subdue them to the useful and the good.
Most blameless is he, centred in the sphere
Of common duties, decent not to fail   40
In offices of tenderness, and pay
Meet adoration to my household gods,
When I am gone. He works his work, I mine.
    There lies the port; the vessel puffs her sail:
There gloom the dark broad seas. My mariners,
Souls that have toil'd, and wrought, and thought with me –
That ever with a frolic welcome took
The thunder and the sunshine, and opposed
Free hearts, free foreheads – you and I are old;
Old age hath yet his honour and his toil;   50
Death closes all: but something ere the end,
Some work of noble note, may yet be done,
Not unbecoming men that strove with Gods.
The lights begin to twinkle from the rocks:
The long day wanes: the slow moon climbs: the deep
Moans round with many voices. Come, my friends,
'Tis not too late to seek a newer world.
Push off, and sitting well in order smite
The sounding furrows; for my purpose holds
To sail beyond the sunset, and the baths   60
Of all the western stars, until I die.
It may be that the gulfs will wash us down:

It may be we shall touch the Happy Isles,
And see the great Achilles, whom we knew.
Tho' much is taken, much abides; and tho'
We are not now that strength which in old days
Moved earth and heaven; that which we are, we are;
One equal temper of heroic hearts,
Made weak by time and fate, but strong in will
To strive, to seek, to find, and not to yield.   70

                                        Alfred, Lord Tennyson

Dulce Et Decorum Est

Bent double, like old beggars under sacks,
Knock-kneed, coughing like hags, we cursed through sludge,
Till on the haunting flares we turned our backs
And towards our distant rest began to trudge.
Men marched asleep. Many had lost their boots
But limped on, blood-shod. All went lame; all blind;
Drunk with fatigue; deaf even to the hoots
Of tired, outstripped Five-Nines[1] that dropped behind.

Gas! Gas! Quick, boys! – An ecstasy of fumbling,
Fitting the clumsy helmets just in time;   10
But someone still was yelling out and stumbling
And flound'ring like a man in fire or lime...
Dim, through the misty panes and thick green light,
As under a green sea, I saw him drowning.

In all my dreams, before my helpless sight,
He plunges at me, guttering, choking, drowning.

If in some smothering dreams you too could pace
Behind the wagon that we flung him in,
And watch the white eyes writhing in his face,
His hanging face, like a devil's sick of sin;   20
If you could hear, at every jolt, the blood
Come gargling from the froth-corrupted lungs,
Obscene as cancer, bitter as the cud
Of vile, incurable sores on innocent tongues, –
My friend, you would not tell with such high zest
To children ardent for some desperate glory,
The old Lie: Dulce et decorum est
Pro patria mori.   *Wilfred Owen*

[1] A much-hated, very destructive German high-explosive shell.

5 Ways to Kill a Man

There are many cumbersome ways to kill a man:
you can make him carry a plank of wood
to the top of a hill and nail him to it. To do this
properly you require a crowd of people
wearing sandals, a cock that crows, a cloak
to dissect, a sponge, some vinegar and one
man to hammer the nails home.

Or you can take a length of steel,
shaped and chased in a traditional way,
and attempt to pierce the metal cage he wears.   10
But for this you need white horses,
English trees, men with bows and arrows,
at least two flags, a prince and a
castle to hold your banquet in.

Dispensing with nobility, you may, if the wind
allows, blow gas at him. But then you need
a mile of mud sliced through with ditches,
not to mention black boots, bomb craters,
more mud, a plague of rats, a dozen songs
and some round hats made of steel.   20

In an age of aeroplanes, you may fly
miles above your victim and dispose of him by
pressing one small switch. All you then
require is an ocean to separate you, two
systems of government, a nation's scientists,
several factories, a psychopath and
land that no one needs for several years.

These are, as I began, cumbersome ways
to kill a man. Simpler, direct, and much more neat
is to see that he is living somewhere in the middle   30
of the twentieth century, and leave him there.

Edwin Brock

The Dam

This was our valley, yes,
Our valley till they came
And chose to build the dam.
All the village worked on it
And we were lucky of course
All through the slump we had
Good jobs; they were too well paid
For the water rose ninety feet,

And covered our houses; yes –
In a midsummer drought   10
The old church-spire pokes out
And the weather cock treads the wind
But we were lucky of course
We were – most of us – laid on
Like the water, to the town.
Somehow, I stayed behind.

I work on the dam, yes –
Do you think the drowned ash-trees
Still have faint impulses
When Spring's up here I wonder?   20
I was lucky of course
But oh there's a lot of me
Feels like a stifled tree
That went on living, under.

They turn on their taps, yes,
In the dusty city and drink:
Now is it that we sink
Or that the waters rise?
They are lucky of course
But as they go to work   30
There's an underwater look
In their Street-shuttered eyes.

This was our valley, yes,
And I live on the dam
And in my sight the dream
Still drowns the dreamer's home
But I am lucky of course
For in a time of drought
Within me and without
I see where I came from.   40

Patric Dickinson

Dockery and Son

'Dockery was junior to you,
Wasn't he?' said the Dean. 'His son's here now.'
Death-suited, visitant, I nod. 'And do
You keep in touch with —' Or remember how
Black-gowned, unbreakfasted, and still half-tight
We used to stand before that desk, to give
'Our version' of 'these incidents last night'?
I try the door of where I used to live:

Locked. The lawn spreads dazzlingly wide.
A known bell chimes. I catch my train, ignored.   10
Canal and clouds and colleges subside
Slowly from view. But Dockery, good Lord,
Anyone up today must have been born
In '43, when I was twenty-one.
If he was younger, did he get this son
At nineteen, twenty? Was he that withdrawn

High-collared public-schoolboy, sharing rooms
With Cartwright who was killed? Well, it just shows
How much...How little...Yawning, I suppose
I fell asleep, waking at the fumes   20
And furnace-glares of Sheffield, where I changed,
And ate an awful pie, and walked along
The platform to its end to see the ranged
Joining and parting lines reflect a strong

Unhindered moon. To have no son, no wife,
No house or land still seemed quite natural.
Only a numbness registered the shock
Of finding out how much had gone of life,
How widely from the others. Dockery, now:
Only nineteen, he must have taken stock   30
Of what he wanted, and been capable
Of... No, that's not the difference: rather, how

Convinced he was he should be added to!
Why did he think adding meant increase?
To me it was dilution. Where do these
Innate assumptions come from? Not from what
We think truest, or most want to do:
Those warp tight-shut, like doors. They're more a style
Our lives bring with them: habit for a while,
Suddenly they harden into all we've got   40

And how we got it; looked back on, they rear
Like sand-clouds, thick and close, embodying
For Dockery a son, for me nothing,
Nothing with all a son's harsh patronage.
Life is first boredom, then fear.
Whether or not we use it, it goes,
And leaves what something hidden from us chose,
And age, and then the only end of age.

Philip Larkin

Adlestrop

Yes. I remember Adlestrop –
The name, because one afternoon
Of heat the express-train drew up there
Unwontedly. It was late June.

The steam hissed. Someone cleared his throat.
No one left and no one came
On the bare platform. What I saw
Was Adlestrop – only the name

And willows, willow-herb, and grass,
And meadowsweet, and haycocks dry,
No whit less still and lonely fair
Than the high cloudlets in the sky.

And for that minute a blackbird sang
Close by, and round him, mistier,
Farther and farther, all the birds
Of Oxfordshire and Gloucestershire.

Edward Thomas

In Praise of Limestone

If it form the one landscape that we the inconstant ones
    Are consistently homesick for, this is chiefly
Because it dissolves in water. Mark these rounded slopes
    With their surface fragrance of thyme and beneath
A secret system of caves and conduits; hear these springs
    That spurt out everywhere with a chuckle
Each filling a private pool for its fish and carving
    Its own little ravine whose cliffs entertain
The butterfly and the lizard; examine this region
    Of short distances and definite places: 10
What could be more like Mother or a fitter background
    For her son, for the nude young male who lounges
Against a rock displaying his dildo, never doubting
    That for all his faults he is loved, whose works are but
Extensions of his power to charm? From weathered outcrop
    To hill-top temple, from appearing waters to
Conspicuous fountains, from a wild to a formal vineyard,
    Are ingenious but short steps that a child's wish
To receive more attention than his brothers, whether
    By pleasing or teasing, can easily take.   20

Watch, then, the band of rivals as they climb up and down
    Their steep stone gennels in twos and threes, sometimes
Arm in arm, but never, thank God, in step; or engaged
    On the shady side of a square at midday in
Voluble discourse, knowing each other too well to think

There are any important secrets, unable
To conceive a god whose temper-tantrums are moral
And not to be pacified by a clever line
Or a good lay: for, accustomed to a stone that responds,
They have never had to veil their faces in awe   30
Of a crater whose blazing fury could not be fixed;
Adjusted to the local needs of valleys
Where everything can be touched or reached by walking,
Their eyes have never looked into infinite space
Through the lattice-work of a nomad's comb; born lucky,
Their legs have never encountered the fungi
And insects of the jungle, the monstrous forms and lives
With which we have nothing, we like to hope, in common.
So, when one of them goes to the bad, the way his mind works
Remains comprehensible: to become a pimp   40
Or deal in fake jewelry or ruin a fine tenor voice
For effects that bring down the house could happen to all
But the best and the worst of us...
                                                That is why, I suppose,
The best and worst never stayed here long but sought
Immoderate soils where the beauty was not so external,
The light less public and the meaning of life
Something more than a mad camp. 'Come!' cried the granite
    wastes,
'How evasive is your humor, how accidental
Your kindest kiss, how permanent is death.' (Saints-to-be   50
Slipped away sighing.) 'Come!' purred the clays and gravels,
'On our plains there is room for armies to drill; rivers
Wait to be tamed and slaves to construct you a tomb
In the grand manner: soft as the earth is mankind and both
Need to be altered.' (Intendant Caesars rose and
Left, slamming the door.) But the really reckless were fetched
By an older colder voice, the oceanic whisper:
'I am the solitude that asks and promises nothing;
That is how I shall set you free. There is no love;
There are only the various envies, all of them sad.'   60

They were right, my dear, all those voices were right
And still are; this land is not the sweet home that it looks,
   Nor its peace the historical calm of a site
Where something was settled once and for all: A backward
   And dilapidated province, connected
To the big busy world by a tunnel, with a certain
   Seedy appeal, is that all it is now? Not quite:
It has a worldly duty which in spite of itself
   It does not neglect, but calls into question
All the Great Powers assume; it disturbs our rights. The poet,   70
   Admired for his earnest habit of calling
The sun the sun, his mind Puzzle, is made uneasy
   By these solid statues which so obviously doubt
His antimythological myth; and these gamins,
   Pursuing the scientist down the tiled colonnade
With such lively offers, rebuke his concern for Nature's
   Remotest aspects: I, too, am reproached, for what
And how much you know. Not to lose time, not to get caught,
   Not to be left behind, not, please! to resemble
The beasts who repeat themselves, or a thing like water   80
   Or stone whose conduct can be predicted, these
Are our Common Prayer, whose greatest comfort is music
   Which can be made anywhere, is invisible,
And does not smell. In so far as we have to look forward
   To death as a fact, no doubt we are right: But if
Sins can be forgiven, if bodies rise from the dead,
   These modifications of matter into
Innocent athletes and gesticulating fountains,
   Made solely for pleasure, make a further point:
The blessed will not care what angle they are regarded from,   90
   Having nothing to hide. Dear, I know nothing of
Either, but when I try to imagine a faultless love
   Or the life to come, what I hear is the murmur
Of underground streams, what I see is a limestone landscape.

                                                  W. H. Auden

The Windhover

To Christ our Lord

I caught this morning morning's minion, king-
   dom of daylight's dauphin, dapple-dawn-drawn Falcon, in his
     riding
Of the rolling level underneath him steady air, and striding
High there, how he rung upon the rein of a wimpling wing
In his ecstasy! then off, off forth on swing,
   As a skate's heel sweeps smooth on a bow-bend: the hurl and
     gliding
Rebuffed the big wind. My heart in hiding
Stirred for a bird, – the achieve of, the mastery of the thing!

Brute beauty and valour and act, oh, air, pride, plume, here
   Buckle! AND the fire that breaks from thee then, a billion
Times told lovelier, more dangerous. O my chevalier!

No wonder of it: shéer plód makes plough down sillion
Shine, and blue-bleak embers, ah my dear,
   Fall, gall themselves, and gash gold-vermilion.

Gerard Manley Hopkins

On first looking into Chapman's Homer

Much have I travell'd in the realms of gold,
   And many goodly states and kingdoms seen;
   Round many western islands have I been
Which bards in fealty to Apollo hold.
Oft of one wide expanse had I been told
   That deep-brow'd Homer ruled as his demesne;
   Yet did I never breathe its pure serene
Till I heard Chapman speak out loud and bold:
Then felt I like some watcher of the skies
   When a new planet swims into his ken;
Or like stout Cortez when with eagle eyes
   He star'd at the Pacific – and all his men
Look'd at each other with a wild surmise –
   Silent, upon a peak in Darien.

John Keats

L'Allegro

Hence, loathèd Melancholy,
  Of Cerberus and blackest Midnight born,
In Stygian cave forlorn
  'Mongst horrid shapes, and shrieks, and sights unholy,
Find out some uncouth cell,
  Where brooding darkness spreads his jealous wings,
And the night-raven sings;
  There under ebon shades and low-browed rocks,
As ragged as thy locks,
  In dark Cimmerian desert ever dwell.   10
But come, thou Goddess fair and free,
In heav'n yclept Euphrosyne,
And by men heart-easing Mirth,
Whom lovely Venus at a birth
With two sister Graces more
To ivy-crownèd Bacchus bore;
Or whether (as some sager sing)
The frolic wind that breathes the spring,
Zephyr, with Aurora playing,
As he met her once a-Maying,   20
There on beds of violets blue,
And fresh-blown roses washed in dew,
Filled her with thee, a daughter fair,
So buxom, blithe, and debonair.
Haste thee, Nymph, and bring with thee
Jest and youthful Jollity,
Quips and Cranks, and wanton Wiles,
Nods and Becks and wreathèd Smiles,
Such as hang on Hebe's cheek,
And love to live in dimple sleek;   30
Sport that wrinkled Care derides,
And Laughter holding both his sides.
Come, and trip it as ye go
On the light fantastic toe,
And in thy right hand lead with thee
The mountain nymph, sweet Liberty;
And if I give thee honor due,
Mirth, admit me of thy crew,
To live with her, and live with thee,

In unreprovèd pleasures free;   40
To hear the lark begin his flight,
And singing startle the dull night,
From his watch-tow'r in the skies,
Till the dappled dawn doth rise;
Then to come in spite of sorrow
And at my window bid good-morrow,
Through the sweet-briar or the vine,
Or the twisted eglantine;
While the cock with lively din
Scatters the rear of darkness thin,   50
And to the stack or the barn door
Stoutly struts his dames before;
Oft list'ning how the hounds and horn
Cheerly rouse the slumb'ring morn,
From the side of some hoar hill,
Through the high wood echoing shrill;
Sometime walking, not unseen,
By hedgerow elms, on hillocks green,
Right against the eastern gate,
Where the great sun begins his state,   60
Robed in flames and amber light,
The clouds in thousand liveries dight;
While the ploughman near at hand
Whistles o'er the furrowed land,
And the milkmaid singeth blithe,
And the mower whets his scythe,
And every shepherd tells his tale
Under the hawthorn in the dale.
Straight mine eye hath caught new pleasures,
Whilst the landscape round it measures: 70
Russet lawns and fallows gray,
Where the nibbling flocks do stray;
Mountains on whose barren breast
The laboring clouds do often rest;
Meadows trim with daisies pied,
Shallow brooks and rivers wide.
Towers and battlements it sees
Bosomed high in tufted trees,
Where perhaps some beauty lies,
The cynosure of neighboring eyes.   80

Hard by, a cottage chimney smokes
From betwixt two aged oaks,
Where Corydon and Thyrsis met
Are at their savory dinner set
Of herbs and other country messes,
Which the neat-handed Phillis dresses;
And then in haste her bow'r she leaves,
With Thestylis to bind the sheaves;
Or if the earlier season lead,
To the tanned haycock in the mead.   90
Sometimes with secure delight
The upland hamlets will invite,
When the merry bells ring round,
And the jocund rebecks sound
To many a youth and many a maid
Dancing in the chequered shade;
And young and old come forth to play
On a sunshine holiday,
Till the livelong daylight fail:
Then to the spicy nut-brown ale,   100
With stories told of many a feat,
How fairy Mab the junkets eat;
She was pinched and pulled, she said,
And he, by friar's lantern led,
Tells how the drudging goblin sweat
To earn his cream-bowl duly set,
When in one night, ere glimpse of morn,
His shadowy flail hath threshed the corn
That ten day-laborers could not end;
Then lies him down the lubber fiend,   110
And stretched out all the chimney's length,
Basks at the fire his hairy strength;
And crop-full out of doors he flings,
Ere the first cock his matin rings.
Thus done the tales, to bed they creep,
By whispering winds soon lulled asleep.
Towered cities please us then,
And the busy hum of men,
Where throngs of knights and barons bold
In weeds of peace high triumphs hold,   120
With store of ladies, whose bright eyes

Rain influence, and judge the prize
Of wit or arms, while both contend
To win her grace whom all commend.
There let Hymen oft appear
In saffron robe, with taper clear,
And pomp, and feast, and revelry,
With masque and antique pageantry:
Such sights as youthful poets dream
On summer eves by haunted stream.   130
Then to the well-trod stage anon,
If Jonson's learned sock be on,
Or sweetest Shakespeare, Fancy's child,
Warble his native wood-notes wild;
And ever against eating cares
Lap me in soft Lydian airs,
Married to immortal verse,
Such as the meeting soul may pierce
In notes with many a winding bout
Of linkèd sweetness long drawn out,   140
With wanton heed and giddy cunning,
The melting voice through mazes running,
Untwisting all the chains that tie
The hidden soul of harmony;
That Orpheus' self may heave his head
From golden slumber on a bed
Of heaped Elysian flow'rs, and hear
Such strains as would have won the ear
Of Pluto, to have quite set free
His half-regained Eurydice.   150
These delights if thou canst give,
Mirth, with thee I mean to live.

John Milton

Wood and Windfall

The fleshy petal
Shivers descendingly to
Moor on the mirror of the wood; fingers of the breeze
Detached it to feather
The sea of the room. A sudden light
And windfall and stillness. Simple as
The act of a good woman
At the pool of her glass, the day dons
Diamonds and drabness flashes.
Flashes. Light-falls. Observe
The lamps of, moons of, their festivals.

Wind falls. Observe
That timber of the usual
Which dreams in the rich yard and
Sweetens with seasoning and
Firms its grain into
Hardwood, heartwood.   *John Holloway*

The Lesson

'Your father's gone,' my bald headmaster said.
His shiny dome and brown tobacco jar
Splintered at once in tears. It wasn't grief.
I cried for knowledge which was bitterer
Than any grief. For there and then I knew
That grief has uses – that a father dead
Could bind the bully's fist a week or two;
And then I cried for shame, then for relief.

I was a month past ten when I learnt this:
I still remember how the noise was stilled
In school-assembly when my grief came in.
Some goldfish in a bowl quietly sculled
Around their shining prison on its shelf.
They were indifferent. All the other eyes
Were turned towards me. Somewhere in myself
Pride, like a goldfish, flashed a sudden fin.

Edward Lucie-Smith

The Place's Fault

Once, after a rotten day at school –
Sweat on my fingers, pages thumbed with smears,
Cane smashing down to make me keep them neat –
I blinked out to the sunlight and the heat
And stumbled up the hill, still swallowing tears.
A stone hissed past my ear – 'Yah! gurt fat fool!'

Some urchins waited for me by my gate.
I shouted swear-words at them, walked away.
'Yeller,' they yelled, ''e's yeller!' And they flung
Clods, stones, bricks – anything to make me run.   10
I ran, all right, up hill all scorching day
With 'yeller' in my ears. 'I'm not, I'm not!'

Another time, playing too near the shops –
Oddly, no doubt, I'm told I was quite odd,
Making, no doubt, a noise – a girl in slacks
Came out and told some kids 'Run round the back,
Bash in his back door, smash up his back yard,
And if he yells I'll go and fetch the cops.'

And what a rush I had to lock those doors
Before that rabble reached them! What desire   20
I've had these twenty years to lock away
That place where fingers pointed out my play,
Where even the grass was tangled with barbed wire,
Where through the streets I waged continual wars!

We left (it was a temporary halt)
The knots of ragged kids, the wired-off beach,
Faces behind the blinds. I'll not return;
There's nothing there I haven't had to learn,
And I've learned nothing that I'd care to teach –
Except that I know it was the place's fault.   30

Philip Hobsbaum

Hawk Roosting

I sit in the top of the wood, my eyes closed.
Inaction, no falsifying dream
Between my hooked head and hooked feet:
Or in sleep rehearse perfect kills and eat.

The convenience of the high trees!
The air's buoyancy and the sun's ray
Are of advantage to me;
And the earth's face upward for my inspection.

My feet are locked upon the rough bark.
It took the whole of Creation   10
To produce my foot, my each feather:
Now I hold Creation in my foot

Or fly up, and revolve it all slowly –
I kill where I please because it is all mine.
There is no sophistry in my body:
My manners are tearing off heads –

The allotment of death.
For the one path of my flight is direct
Through the bones of the living.
No arguments assert my right: 20

The sun is behind me.
Nothing has changed since I began.
My eye has permitted no change.
I am going to keep things like this.

Ted Hughes

Sonnet

I wish I could remember that first day, *a*
First hour, first moment of your meeting me, *b*
If bright or dim the season, it might be *b*
Summer or Winter for aught I can say; *a*
So unrecorded did it slip away, *c*
So blind was I to see and to foresee, *d*
So dull to mark the budding of my tree *d*
That would not blossom yet for many a May. *c*
If only I could recollect it, such *e*
A day of days! I let it come and go *f*
As traceless as a thaw of bygone snow; *f*
It seemed to mean so little, meant so much; *g*
If only now I could recall that touch *g*
First touch of hand in hand – Did one but know! *f*

Christina Rossetti

Iambic
Pentameter

Western Wind

Western wind, when will thou blow,
   The small rain down can rain?
Christ, if my love were in my arms
   And I in my bed again!

Anonymous

126

I am the only being whose doom

I am the only being whose doom
No tongue would ask, no eye would mourn;
I never caused a thought of gloom,
A smile of joy, since I was born.

In secret pleasure, secret tears,
This changeful life has slipped away,
As friendless after eighteen years,
As lone as on my natal day.

There have been times I cannot hide,
There have been times when this was drear,   10
When my sad soul forgot its pride
And longed for one to love me here.

But those were in the early glow
Of feelings since subdued by care,
And they have died so long ago
I hardly now believe they were.

First melted off the hope of youth,
Then fancy's rainbow fast withdrew,
And then experience told me truth
In mortal bosoms never grew.   20

'Twas grief enough to think mankind
All hollow, servile, insincere –
But worse to trust to my own mind
And find the same corruption there.

                    Emily Brontë

My Blue Heaven

I thought it was a Glue Factory –
a whiff of boiled bones
and the knacker's yard

excreted in the lee of the fells.
The smell of desperate exhumations
briefly fills the car.

I was wrong, the wind flicking
the plosive back into the throat:
it's the *Blue* Factory

staining the air, staining   10
the village beck, leaving
its cobalt drift of talcum

on window-sill and ledge,
tinting the grey-green slate
with hints of early Picasso.

The factory chimney steams
like a pencil designing fumes.
All this to manufacture Blue:

that stuff to make the sheets gleam
bright in a glossy commercial,   20
the stuff they use to justify

the suburbs' aerial madness.
As the ferro-cyanic stench
recedes, I wonder what

strange manufacturer
makes all the distant stuff
that gives some inflated clouds

their whiter than cotton whiteness?
What heavenly smell, pray,
lies behind all *that*?   30

Rodney Pybus

WRITING ESSAYS IN CLASS

The main difference between writing essays in class and writing them in exams is that in class (or at home) you usually have the text available. This means you can look up any quotation you need and there is less emphasis on actual recall of the poem.

In some cases you might also be given the opportunity to re-write an essay which you have not managed satisfactorily at the first attempt – an advantage never available in an examination.

When preparing for an essay which is to be written in class or at home you ought to concentrate on making the lines of your argument clear. Since knowledge of the text is regarded differently if you have the book in front of you, there are two aspects in your course-work which it is important to show:

(a) your ability to marshal the text to the purposes of your argument;

(b) your comments upon the text which heighten (or explain in detail) the effects of the particular words, phrases, lines you refer to.

Usually the point of asking students to write an essay as part of their course-work is to encourage them to see connections between poems and to enable them to distinguish and differentiate between styles and approaches to writing poetry. This is why essay titles often invite you to write on several poems which deal with similar subjects, or which are written in the same form (such as the sonnet).

So you might be required to write, for instance, on the attitude to childhood of at least three poets in your selection; or on the treatment of the town or country; or on the treatment of love, or death, or joy, or pain. It will occur to you as you read through any section of this anthology that there are connections which can be made between many of the poems in it.

If your answer concentrates on the main differences of attitude from poet to poet, and then shows how each attitude is made clear by the particular choice of phrasing, image, or rhythm in each poem you discuss, then your answer should fulfil the requirements of the question.

Your own emphasis in the statements you make will determine how successful your essay is. For this reason you must be clear and positive in everything you say. This is especially so as you move from one paragraph to another in your essay, or from one poem to another.

129

Look at the two poems about old age which are printed below:

I look into my glass,
And view my wasting skin,
And say, 'Would God it came to pass
My heart had shrunk as thin!'

For then, I, undistrest
By hearts grown cold to me,
Could lonely wait my endless rest
With equanimity.

But Time, to make me grieve,
Part steals, lets part abide;
And shakes this fragile frame at eve
With throbbings of noontide.

Thomas Hardy

Beautiful Old Age

It ought to be lovely to be old
to be full of the peace that comes of experience
and wrinkled ripe fulfilment.

The wrinkled smile of completeness that follows a life
lived undaunted and unsoured with accepted lies.
If people lived without accepting lies
they would ripen like apples, and be scented like pippins
in their old age.

Soothing, old people should be, like apples
when one is tired of love.
Fragrant like yellowing leaves, and dim with the soft
stillness and satisfaction of autumn.

And a girl should say:
It must be wonderful to live and grow old.
Look at my mother, how rich and still she is! –

And a young man should think: By Jove
my father has faced all weathers, but it's been a life! –

D. H. Lawrence

Suppose you were writing an essay on different treatments of old age, using these two poems. There are clearly many differences in the treatment you would want to mention:

Difference in attitude
Hardy: regrets being old
Lawrence: thinks it should bring a sense of fulfilment

Point of view
Hardy: writes as an old man
Lawrence: writes of an experience he has not had

Poetic form
Hardy: carefully crafts his poem, using rhymes and regular rhythm
Lawrence: seems spontaneous, almost conversational, as if he is writing at the same speed as he thinks

The important thing is to make the opening sentence of each paragraph state clearly what the point of the paragraph is, and how it follows from what you have already said. Notice the emphases and connections in the essay below:

Hardy's poem is a poem written by an old man who begins by looking into a mirror and reacting to what he sees – his 'wasting skin'. This is what starts him thinking about his old age. It is not clear what makes Lawrence begin his thoughts on old age. He just seems to leap straight into the question.

Possibly Lawrence has a point to prove, and he is using old age to prove it. He seems mainly concerned with 'accepted lies', although he never says what these are – which makes it difficult to understand exactly what he is getting at. Lawrence is confusing when he says that

'If people lived without accepting lies
they would ripen like apples, and be scented like pippins
in their old age.'

The only thing I can think of that he might mean is that the smell of apples is fresh whereas a dishonest life sours you.

Lawrence's poem is made even more difficult to follow when he refers to being tired of love. I cannot really see the connection between apples and 'when one is tired of love'. Perhaps he means that love is a very important thing in life and that after it has gone there is still a sense of freshness. Some people think that old people have nothing they can be interested in.

Thomas Hardy shows that old people are still interested in emotions like love – 'throbbings of noontide' – which distress them because they are still able to feel hurt. Old people are often neglected because their bodies are aged, even though their minds remain lively. If they did not have lively minds and emotions then they would not worry about being neglected – Hardy could 'lonely wait my endless rest with equanimity'. The word 'equanimity' is long and smooth. It takes up almost the whole line by itself, and because it fits so perfectly into

131

the rhythm of the poem it sounds like the smooth and undisturbed mood which Hardy would like to have. It is typical of the careful rhythm of the poem, which also has a regular rhyme scheme. This makes the poem seem very carefully thought out. But Lawrence's poem does not have any of this care. The references to what a girl or a young man should say about their parents at the end of the poem look like afterthoughts, and they do not have anything to say about apples or lies.

Lawrence's lines do not have any rhymes and they are all different lengths, as if he does not really want it to look like a poem, or perhaps it is an idea for a poem which he never got round to completing. This might be because he had no real reason for writing about the subject. He was not an old man himself and he was only guessing what it would be like. He says that 'it ought to be lovely to be old', which might mean that he thinks it probably isn't. He treats old people as things to be thought about by other people, but Hardy was more involved with actually being old because he had the 'fragile frame' which was shaken by strong youthful emotions.

SECTION E:

'Fill all fruit with ripeness to the core'

Mid-Term Break

I sat all morning in the college sick bay
Counting bells knelling classes to a close.
At two o'clock our neighbours drove me home.

In the porch I met my father crying –
He had always taken funerals in his stride –
And Big Jim Evans saying it was a hard blow.

The baby cooed and laughed and rocked the pram
When I came in, and I was embarrassed
By old men standing up to shake my hand

And tell me they were 'sorry for my trouble',   10
Whispers informed strangers I was the eldest,
Away at school, as my mother held my hand

In hers and coughed out angry tearless sighs.
At ten o'clock the ambulance arrived
With the corpse, stanched and bandaged by the nurses.

Next morning I went up into the room. Snowdrops
And candles soothed the bedside; I saw him
For the first time in six weeks. Paler now,

Wearing a poppy bruise on his left temple,
He lay in the four foot box as in his cot.   20
No gaudy scars, the bumper knocked him clear.

A four foot box, a foot for every year.

Seamus Heaney

Snake

A snake came to my water-trough
On a hot, hot day, and I in pyjamas for the heat,
To drink there.

In the deep, strange-scented shade of the great dark carob-tree
I came down the steps with my pitcher
And must wait, must stand and wait, for there he was at the
    trough before me.

He reached down from a fissure in the earthwall in the gloom
And trailed his yellow-brown slackness soft-bellied down, over
    the edge of the stone trough
And rested his throat upon the stone bottom,
And where the water had dripped from the tap, in a small
    clearness,   10
He sipped with his straight mouth,
Softly drank through his straight gums, into his slack long body,
Silently.

Someone was before me at my water-trough,
And I, like a second comer, waiting.

He lifted his head from his drinking, as cattle do,
And looked at me vaguely, as drinking cattle do,
And flickered his two-forked tongue from his lips, and mused a
    moment,
And stopped and drank a little more,
Being earth-brown, earth-golden from the burning bowels of the
    earth   20
On the day of Sicilian July, with Etna smoking.

The voice of my education said to me
He must be killed,
For in Sicily the black, black snakes are innocent, the gold are
    venomous.

And voices in me said, If you were a man
You would take a stick and break him now, and finish him off.

But must I confess how I liked him,
How glad I was he had come like a guest in quiet, to drink at
    my water-trough
And depart peaceful, pacified, and thankless,
Into the burning bowels of this earth?   30

Was it cowardice, that I dared not kill him?
Was it perversity, that I longed to talk to him?
Was it humility, to feel so honoured?
I felt so honoured.

And yet those voices:
If you were not afraid, you would kill him!

And truly I was afraid, I was most afraid,
But even so, honoured still more
That he should seek my hospitality
From out the dark door of the secret earth.   40

He drank enough
And lifted his head, dreamily, as one who has drunken,
And flickered his tongue like a forked night on the air, so black,
Seeming to lick his lips,
And looked around like a god, unseeing, into the air,
And slowly turned his head,
And slowly, very slowly, as if thrice adream,
Proceeded to draw his slow length curving round
And climb again the broken bank of my wall-face.

And as he put his head into that dreadful hole,   50
And as he slowly drew up, snake-easing his shoulders, and
    entered farther,
A sort of horror, a sort of protest against his withdrawing, into
    that horrid black hole,
Deliberately going into the blackness, and slowly drawing
    himself after,
Overcame me now his back was turned.

I looked round, I put down my pitcher,
I picked up a clumsy log
And threw it at the water-trough with a clatter.

I think it did not hit him,
But suddenly that part of him that was left behind convulsed in
    undignified haste,
Writhed like lightning, and was gone   60
Into the black hole, the earth-lipped fissure in the wall-front,
At which, in the intense still noon, I stared with fascination.

And immediately I regretted it.
I thought how paltry, how vulgar, what a mean act!
I despised myself and the voices of my accursed human
    education.

And I thought of the albatross,
And I wished he would come back, my snake.

For he seemed to me again like a king,
Like a king in exile, uncrowned in the underworld,
Now due to be crowned again.   70

And so, I missed my chance with one of the lords
Of life.
And I have something to expiate;
A pettiness.   *D. H. Lawrence*

Dover Beach

The sea is calm to-night.
The tide is full, the moon lies fair
Upon the straits; – on the French coast the light
Gleams and is gone; the cliffs of England stand,
Glimmering and vast, out in the tranquil bay.
Come to the window, sweet is the night-air!
Only, from the long line of spray
Where the sea meets the moon-blanch'd land,
Listen! you hear the grating roar
Of pebbles which the waves draw back, and fling,   10
At their return, up the high strand,
Begin, and cease, and then again begin,
With tremulous cadence slow, and bring
The eternal note of sadness in.

Sophocles long ago
Heard it on the Aegean, and it brought
Into his mind the turbid ebb and flow
Of human misery; we
Find also in the sound a thought,
Hearing it by this distant northern sea.　　　　　20

The Sea of Faith
Was once, too, at the full, and round earth's shore
Lay like the folds of a bright girdle furl'd.
But now I only hear
Its melancholy, long, withdrawing roar,
Retreating, to the breath
Of the night-wind, down the vast edges drear
And naked shingles of the world.

Ah, love, let us be true
To one another! for the world, which seems　　　　30
To lie before us like a land of dreams,
So various, so beautiful, so new,
Hath really neither joy, nor love, nor light,
Nor certitude, nor peace, nor help for pain;
And we are here as on a darkling plain
Swept with confused alarms of struggle and flight,
Where ignorant armies clash by night.　　　*Matthew Arnold*

On My First Sonne

Farewell, thou child of my right hand, and joy;
　　My sinne was too much hope of thee, lov'd boy,
Seven yeeres tho'wert lent to me, and I thee pay,
　　Exacted by thy fate, on the just day.
O, could I loose all father, now. For why
　　Will man lament the state he should envie?
To have so soone scap'd worlds, and fleshes rage,
　　And, if no other miserie, yet age?
Rest in soft peace, and, ask'd, say here doth lye
　　BEN JONSON his best piece of *poetrie*.
For whose sake, hence-forth, all his vowes be such,
　　As what he loves may never like too much.　　　*Ben Jonson*

137

Refugee Mother and Child

No Madonna and Child could touch
that picture of a mother's tenderness
for a son she soon would have to forget.

The air was heavy with odours
of diarrhoea of unwashed children
with washed-out ribs and dried-up
bottoms struggling in laboured
steps behind blown empty bellies. Most
mothers there had long ceased
to care but not this one; she held   10
a ghost smile between her teeth
and in her eyes the ghost of a mother's
pride as she combed the rust-coloured
hair left on his skull and then –
singing in her eyes – began carefully
to part it...In another life this
would have been a little daily
act of no consequence before his
breakfast and school; now she
did it like putting flowers   20
on a tiny grave.

                              Chinua Achebe

A Refusal to Mourn the Death, by Fire, of a Child in London

Never until the mankind making
Bird beast and flower
Fathering and all humbling darkness
Tells with silence the last light breaking
And the still hour
Is come of the sea tumbling in harness

And I must enter again the round
Zion of the water bead
And the synagogue of the ear of corn
Shall I let pray the shadow of a sound   10
Or sow my salt seed
In the least valley of sackcloth to mourn

The majesty and burning of the child's death.
I shall not murder
The mankind of her going with a grave truth
Nor blaspheme down the stations of the breath
With any further
Elegy of innocence and youth.

Deep with the first dead lies London's daughter,
Robed in the long friends,   20
The grains beyond age, the dark veins of her mother,
Secret by the unmourning water
Of the riding Thames.
After the first death, there is no other.

Dylan Thomas

Prayer before Birth

I am not yet born; O hear me.
Let not the bloodsucking bat or the rat or the stoat or
    the club-footed ghoul come near me.

I am not yet born; console me.
I fear that the human race may with tall walls wall me,
    with strong drugs dope me, with wise lies lure me,
        on black racks rack me, in blood-baths roll me.

I am not yet born; provide me
With water to dandle me, grass to grow for me, tree to talk
    to me, sky to sing to me, birds and a white light
        in the back of my mind to guide me.

I am not yet born; forgive me
For the sins that in me the world shall commit, my words
   when they speak me, my thoughts when they think me,
    my treason engendered by traitors beyond me,
     my life when they murder by means of my
      hands, my death when they live me.

I am not yet born; rehearse me
In the parts I must play and the cues I must take when
old men lecture me, bureaucrats hector me,
   mountains frown on me, lovers laugh at me, the
    white waves call me to folly and the desert calls
     me to doom and the beggar refuses
      my gift and my children curse me.

I am not yet born; O hear me,
Let not the man who is beast or who thinks he is God
   come near me.

I am not yet born; O fill me
With strength against those who would freeze my
   humanity, would dragoon me into a lethal automaton,
    would make me a cog in a machine, a thing with
     one face, a thing, and against all those
      who would dissipate my entirety, would
       blow me like thistledown hither and
        thither or hither and thither
         like water held in the
          hands would spill me.

Let them not make a stone and let them not spill me.
Otherwise kill me.

Louis MacNeice

Poem in October

It was my thirtieth year to heaven
Woke to my hearing from harbour and neighbour wood
  And the mussel pooled and the heron
     Priested shore
    The morning beckon
With water praying and call of seagull and rook
And the knock of sailing boats on the net webbed wall
    Myself to set foot
     That second
  In the still sleeping town and set forth.   10

My birthday began with the water-
Birds and the birds of the winged trees flying my name
  Above the farms and the white horses
     And I rose
    In rainy autumn
And walked abroad in a shower of all my days.
High tide and the heron dived when I took the road
    Over the border
     And the gates
  Of the town closed as the town awoke.   20

A springful of larks in a rolling
Cloud and the roadside bushes brimming with whistling
  Blackbirds and the sun of October
     Summery
    On the hill's shoulder,
Here were fond climates and sweet singers suddenly
Come in the morning where I wandered and listened
    To the rain wringing
     Wind blow cold
  In the wood faraway under me.   30

Pale rain over the dwindling harbour
And over the sea wet church the size of a snail
  With its horns through mist and the castle
     Brown as owls
    But all the gardens
Of spring and summer were blooming in the tall tales

Beyond the border and under the lark full cloud.
    There could I marvel
        My birthday
    Away but the weather turned around.   40

It turned away from the blithe country
And down the other air and the blue altered sky
    Streamed again a wonder of summer
        With apples
        Pears and red currants
And I saw in the turning so clearly a child's
Forgotten mornings when he walked with his mother
        Through the parables
            Of sun light
And the legends of the green chapels.   50

And the twice told fields of infancy
That his tears burned my cheeks and his heart moved in mine.
    These were the woods the river and sea
        Where a boy
        In the listening
Summertime of the dead whispered the truth of his joy
To the trees and the stones and the fish in the tide.
        And the mystery
            Sang alive
Still in the water and singingbirds.   60

And there could I marvel my birthday
Away but the weather turned around. And the true
    Joy of the long dead child sang burning
        In the sun.
    It was my thirtieth
Year to heaven stood there then in the summer noon
Though the town below lay leaved with October blood.
        O may my heart's truth
            Still be sung
On this high hill in a year's turning.   70

                                        Dylan Thomas

To Autumn

Season of mists and mellow fruitfulness,
  Close bosom-friend of the maturing sun;
Conspiring with him how to load and bless
  With fruit the vines that round the thatch-eaves run;
To bend with apples the mossed cottage-trees,
  And fill all fruit with ripeness to the core;
    To swell the gourd, and plump the hazel shells
With a sweet kernel; to set budding more,
And still more, later flowers for the bees,
  Until they think warm days will never cease;   10
    For Summer has o'erbrimmed their clammy cells.

Who hath not seen thee oft amid thy store?
  Sometimes whoever seeks abroad may find
Thee sitting careless on a granary floor,
  Thy hair soft-lifted by the winnowing wind;
Or on a half-reaped furrow sound asleep,
  Drowsed with the fume of poppies, while thy hook
    Spares the next swath and all its twinèd flowers;
And sometimes like a gleaner thou dost keep
  Steady thy laden head across a brook;   20
  Or by a cider-press, with patient look,
    Thou watchest the last oozings, hours by hours.

Where are the songs of Spring? Ay, where are they?
  Think not of them, thou hast thy music too, –
While barrèd clouds bloom the soft-dying day
  And touch the stubble-plains with rosy hue;
Then in a wailful choir the small gnats mourn
  Among the river sallows, borne aloft
    Or sinking as the light wind lives or dies;
And full-grown lambs loud bleat from hilly bourn;   30
  Hedge-crickets sing; and now with treble soft
  The red-breast whistles from a garden-croft,
    And gathering swallows twitter in the skies.

John Keats

Season

Rust is ripeness, rust,
And the wilted corn-plume.
Pollen is mating-time when swallows
Weave a dance
Of feathered arrows
Thread corn-stalks in winged
Streaks of light. And we loved to hear
Spliced phrases of the wind, to hear
Rasps in the field, where corn-leaves
Pierce like bamboo slivers.

Now, garnerers we,
Awaiting rust on tassels, draw
Long shadows from the dusk, wreathe
The thatch in wood-smoke. Laden stalks
Ride the germ's decay – we await
The promise of the rust.

Wole Soyinka

Composed upon Westminster Bridge

Earth has not anything to show more fair:
Dull would he be of soul who could pass by
A sight so touching in its majesty:
This City now doth like a garment wear
The beauty of the morning; silent, bare,
Ships, towers, domes, theatres, and temples lie
Open unto the fields, and to the sky;
All bright and glittering in the smokeless air.
Never did sun more beautifully steep
In his first splendour, valley, rock, or hill;
Ne'er saw I, never felt, a calm so deep!
The river glideth at his own sweet will:
Dear God! the very houses seem asleep;
And all that mighty heart is lying still!

William Wordsworth

As kingfishers catch fire

As kingfishers catch fire, dragonflies draw flame;
As tumbled over rim in roundy wells
Stones ring; like each tucked string tells, each hung bell's
Bow swung finds tongue to fling out broad its name;
Each mortal thing does one thing and the same:
Deals out that being indoors each one dwells;
Selves – goes itself; *myself* it speaks and spells;
Crying *What I do is me: for that I came.*

I say more: the just man justices;
Keeps grace: that keeps all his goings graces;
Acts in God's eye what in God's eye he is –
Christ – for Christ plays in ten thousand places,
Lovely in limbs, and lovely in eyes not his
To the Father through the features of men's faces.

Gerard Manley Hopkins

Preludes

I

The winter evening settles down
With smell of steaks in passageways.
Six o'clock.
The burnt-out ends of smoky days.
And now a gusty shower wraps
The grimy scraps
Of withered leaves about your feet
And newspapers from vacant lots;
The showers beat
On broken blinds and chimney-pots,   10
And at the corner of the street
A lonely cab-horse steams and stamps.
And then the lighting of the lamps.

II

The morning comes to consciousness
Of faint stale smells of beer
From the sawdust-trampled street
With all its muddy feet that press
To early coffee-stands.

With the other masquerades
That time resumes,   20
One thinks of all the hands
That are raising dingy shades
In a thousand furnished rooms.

III

You tossed a blanket from the bed,
You lay upon your back, and waited;
You dozed, and watched the night revealing
The thousand sordid images
Of which your soul was constituted;
They flickered against the ceiling.
And when all the world came back   30
And the light crept up between the shutters
And you heard the sparrows in the gutters,
You had such a vision of the street
As the street hardly understands;
Sitting along the bed's edge, where
You curled the papers from your hair,
Or clasped the yellow soles of feet
In the palms of both soiled hands.

IV

His soul stretched tight across the skies
That fade behind a city block,   40
Or trampled by insistent feet
At four and five and six o'clock;
And short square fingers stuffing pipes,
And even newspapers, and eyes
Assured of certain certainties,
The conscience of a blackened street
Impatient to assume the world.

I am moved by fancies that are curled
Around these images, and cling:
The notion of some infinitely gentle   50
Infinitely suffering thing.

Wipe your hand across your mouth, and laugh;
The worlds revolve like ancient women
Gathering fuel in vacant lots.

                                        T. S. Eliot

Horses

Those lumbering horses in the steady plough,
On the bare field – I wonder why, just now,
They seemed terrible, so wild and strange,
Like magic power on the stony grange.

Perhaps some childish hour has come again,
When I watched fearful, through the blackening rain,
Their hooves like pistons in an ancient mill
Move up and down, yet seem as standing still.

Their conquering hooves which trod the stubble down
Were ritual that turned the field to brown,   10
And their great hulks were seraphim of gold,
Or mute ecstatic monsters on the mould.

And oh the rapture, when, one furrow done,
They marched broad-breasted to the sinking sun!
The light flowed off their bossy sides in flakes;
The furrows rolled behind like struggling snakes.

But when at dusk with steaming nostrils home
They came, they seemed gigantic in the gloam,
And warm and glowing with mysterious fire
That lit their smouldering bodies in the mire.   20

Their eyes as brilliant and as wide as night
Gleamed with a cruel apocalyptic light.
Their manes the leaping ire of the wind
Lifted with rage invisible and blind.

Ah, now it fades! it fades! and I must pine
Again for that dread country crystalline,
Where the blank field and the still-standing tree
Were bright and fearful presences to me.

Edwin Muir

Vitae Lampada

There's a breathless hush in the Close tonight –
Ten to make and the match to win –
A bumping pitch and a blinding light,
An hour to play and the last man in.
And it's not for the sake of a ribboned coat,
Or the selfish hope of a season's fame,
But his Captain's hand on his shoulder smote –
    'Play up! play up! and play the game!'

The sand of the desert is sodden red –
Red with the wreck of a square that broke;   10
The Gatling's jammed and the Colonel dead,
And the Regiment blind with dust and smoke.
The river of death has brimmed his banks,
And England's far and Honour a name,
But the voice of a schoolboy rallies the ranks:
    'Play up! play up! and play the game!'

This is the word that year by year,
While in her place the School is set,
Every one of her sons must hear,
And none that hears it dare forget.   20
This they all with a joyful mind
Bear through life like a torch in flame,
And falling fling to the host behind –
    'Play up! play up! and play the game!'

Sir Henry Newbolt

Andrea del Sarto

(Called 'The Faultless Painter')

But do not let us quarrel any more,
No, my Lucrezia; bear with me for once:
Sit down and all shall happen as you wish.
You turn your face, but does it bring your heart?
I'll work then for your friend's friend, never fear.
Treat his own subject after his own way,

148

Fix his own time, accept too his own price,
And shut the money into this small hand
When next it takes mine. Will it? tenderly?
Oh, I'll content him, – but to-morrow, Love!   10
I often am much wearier than you think,
This evening more than usual, and it seems
As if – forgive now – should you let me sit
Here by the window with your hand in mine
And look a half-hour forth on Fiesole,
Both of one mind, as married people use,
Quietly, quietly, the evening through,
I might get up to-morrow to my work
Cheerful and fresh as ever. Let us try.
To-morrow how you shall be glad for this!   20
Your soft hand is a woman of itself,
And mine the man's bared breast she curls inside.
Don't count the time lost, either; you must serve
For each of the five pictures we require –
It saves a model. So! keep looking so –
My serpentining beauty, rounds on rounds!
– How could you ever prick those perfect ears,
Even to put the pearl there! oh, so sweet –
My face, my moon, my everybody's moon,
Which everybody looks on and calls his,   30
And, I suppose, is looked on by in turn,
While she looks – no one's: very dear, no less!
You smile? why, there's my picture ready made.
There's what we painters call our harmony!
A common greyness silvers everything, –
All in a twilight, you and I alike
– You, at the point of your first pride in me
(That's gone, you know), – but I, at every point;
My youth, my hope, my art, being all toned down
To yonder sober pleasant Fiesole.   40
There's the bell clinking from the chapel-top;
That length of convent-wall across the way
Holds the trees safer, huddled more inside;
The last monk leaves the garden; days decrease
And autumn grows, autumn in everything.
Eh? the whole seems to fall into a shape
As if I saw alike my work and self

And all that I was born to be and do,
A twilight-piece. Love, we are in God's hand.
How strange now, looks the life He makes us lead!　　　50
So free we seem, so fettered fast we are!
I feel He laid the fetter: let it lie!
This chamber for example – turn your head –
All that's behind us! you don't understand
Nor care to understand about my art,
But you can hear at least when people speak;
And that cartoon, the second from the door
– It is the thing, Love! so such things should be –
Behold Madonna, I am bold to say.
I can do with my pencil what I know,　　　60
What I see, what at bottom of my heart
I wish for, if I ever wish so deep –
Do easily, too – when I say perfectly
I do not boast, perhaps: yourself are judge
Who listened to the Legate's talk last week,
And just as much they used to say in France.
At any rate 'tis easy, all of it,
No sketches first, no studies, that's long past –
I do what many dream of all their lives
– Dream? strive to do, and agonise to do,　　　70
And fail in doing. I could count twenty such
On twice your fingers, and not leave this town,
Who strive – you don't know how the others strive
To paint a little thing like that you smeared
Carelessly passing with your robes afloat, –
Yet do much less, so much less, Someone says,
(I know his name, no matter) so much less!
Well, less is more, Lucrezia! I am judged.
There burns a truer light of God in them,
In their vexed, beating, stuffed and stopped-up brain,　　　80
Heart, or whate'er else, than goes on to prompt
This low-pulsed forthright craftsman's hand of mine.
Their works drop groundward, but themselves, I know,
Reach many a time a heaven that's shut to me,
Enter and take their place there sure enough,
Though they come back and cannot tell the world.
My works are nearer heaven, but I sit here.
The sudden blood of these men! at a word –

Praise them, it boils, or blame them, it boils too.
I, painting from myself and to myself, 90
Know what I do, am unmoved by men's blame
Or their praise either. Somebody remarks
Morello's outline there is wrongly traced,
His hue mistaken – what of that? or else,
Rightly traced and well ordered – what of that?
Speak as they please, what does the mountain care?
Ah, but a man's reach should exceed his grasp,
Or what's a Heaven for? all is silver-grey
Placid and perfect with my art – the worse!
I know both what I want and what might gain – 100
And yet how profitless to know, to sigh
'Had I been two, another and myself,
Our head would have o'erlooked the world!' No doubt,
Yonder's a work, now, of that famous youth
The Urbinate who died five years ago.
('Tis copied, George Vasari sent it me.)
Well, I can fancy how he did it all,
Pouring his soul, with kings and popes to see,
Reaching, that Heaven might so replenish him,
Above and through his art – for it gives way; 110
That arm is wrongly put – and there again –
A fault to pardon in the drawing's lines,
Its body, so to speak: its soul is right,
He means right – that, a child may understand.
Still, what an arm! and I could alter it.
But all the play, the insight and the stretch –
Out of me! out of me! And wherefore out?
Had you enjoined them on me, given me soul,
We might have risen to Rafael, I and you.
Nay, Love, you did give all I asked, I think – 120
More than I merit, yes, by many times.
But had you – oh, with the same perfect brow,
And perfect eyes, and more than perfect mouth,
And the low voice my soul hears, as a bird
The fowler's pipe, and follows to the snare –
Had you, with these the same, but brought a mind!
Some women do so. Had the mouth there urged
'God and the glory! never care for gain.
The Present by the Future, what is that?

Live for fame, side by side with Agnolo –   130
Rafael is waiting. Up to God all three!'
I might have done it for you. So it seems –
Perhaps not. All is as God overrules.
Beside, incentives come from the soul's self;
The rest avail not. Why do I need you?
What wife had Rafael, or has Agnolo?
In this world, who can do a thing, will not –
And who would do it, cannot, I perceive:
Yet the will's somewhat – somewhat, too, the power –
And thus we half-men struggle. At the end,   140
God, I conclude, compensates, punishes.
'Tis safe for me, if the award be strict,
That I am something underrated here,
Poor this long while, despised, to speak the truth.
I dared not, do you know, leave home all day,
For fear of chancing on the Paris lords.
The best is when they pass and look aside;
But they speak sometimes; I must bear it all.
Well may they speak! That Francis, that first time,
And that long festal year at Fontainebleau!   150
I surely then could sometimes leave the ground,
Put on the glory, Rafael's daily wear,
In that humane great monarch's golden look, –
One finger in his beard or twisted curl
Over his mouth's good mark that made the smile,
One arm about my shoulder, round my neck,
The jingle of his gold chain in my ear,
I painting proudly with his breath on me,
All his court round him, seeing with his eyes,
Such frank French eyes, and such a fire of souls   160
Profuse, my hand kept plying by those hearts, –
And, best of all, this, this, this face beyond,
This in the background, waiting on my work,
To crown the issue with a last reward!
A good time, was it not, my kingly days?
And had you not grown restless – but I know –
'Tis done and past; 'twas right, my instinct said;
Too live the life grew, golden and not grey,
And I'm the weak-eyed bat no sun should tempt
Out of the grange whose four walls make his world.   170

How could it end in any other way?
You called me, and I came home to your heart.
The triumph was, to have ended there; then if
I reached it ere the triumph, what is lost?
Let my hands frame your face in your hair's gold,
You beautiful Lucrezia that are mine!
  'Rafael did this, Andrea painted that –
The Roman's is the better when you pray,
But still the other's Virgin was his wife – '
Men will excuse me. I am glad to judge   180
Both pictures in your presence; clearer grows
My better fortune, I resolve to think.
For, do you know, Lucrezia, as God lives,
Said one day Agnolo, his very self,
To Rafael...I have known it all these years...
(When the young man was flaming out his thoughts
Upon a palace-wall for Rome to see,
Too lifted up in heart because of it)
'Friend, there's a certain sorry little scrub
Goes up and down our Florence, none cares how,   190
Who, were he set to plan and execute
As you are, pricked on by your popes and kings,
Would bring the sweat into that brow of yours!'
To Rafael's! – And indeed the arm is wrong.
I hardly dare – yet, only you to see,
Give the chalk here – quick, thus the line should go!
Aye, but the soul! he's Rafael! rub it out!
Still, all I care for, if he spoke the truth,
(What he? why, who but Michael Agnolo?
Do you forget already words like those?)   200
If really there was such a chance, so lost, –
Is, whether you're – not grateful – but more pleased.
Well, let me think so. And you smile indeed!
This hour has been an hour! Another smile?
If you would sit thus by me every night
I should work better, do you comprehend?
I mean that I should earn more, give you more.
See, it is settled dusk now; there's a star;
Morello's gone, the watch-lights show the wall,
The cue-owls speak the name we call them by.   210
Come from the window, Love, – come in, at last,

Inside the melancholy little house
We built to be so gay with. God is just.
King Francis may forgive me. Oft at nights
When I look up from painting, eyes tired out,
The walls become illumined, brick from brick
Distinct, instead of mortar, fierce bright gold,
That gold of his I did cement them with!
Let us but love each other. Must you go?
That Cousin here again? he waits outside?   220
Must see you – you, and not with me? Those loans?
More gaming debts to pay? you smiled for that?
Well, let smiles buy me! have you more to spend?
While hand and eye and something of a heart
Are left me, work's my ware, and what's it worth?
I'll pay my fancy. Only let me sit
The grey remainder of the evening out,
Idle, you call it, and muse perfectly
How I could paint, were I but back in France,
One picture, just one more – the Virgin's face,   230
Not yours this time! I want you at my side
To hear them – that is, Michael Agnolo –
Judge all I do and tell you of its worth.
Will you? To-morrow, satisfy your friend.
I take the subjects for his corridor,
Finish the portrait out of hand – there, there,
And throw him in another thing or two
If he demurs; the whole should prove enough
To pay for this same Cousin's freak. Beside,
What's better and what's all I care about,   240
Get you the thirteen scudi for the ruff.
Love, does that please you? Ah, but what does he,
The Cousin! what does he to please you more?

    I am grown peaceful as old age to-night.
I regret little, I would change still less.
Since there my past life lies, why alter it?
The very wrong to Francis! – it is true
I took his coin, was tempted and complied,
And built this house and sinned, and all is said.
My father and my mother died of want.   250
Well, had I riches of my own? you see

154

How one gets rich! Let each one bear his lot.
They were born poor, lived poor, and poor they died:
And I have laboured somewhat in my time
And not been paid profusely. Some good son
Paint my two hundred pictures – let him try!
No doubt, there's something strikes a balance. Yes,
You loved me quite enough, it seems to-night.
This must suffice me here. What would one have?
In Heaven, perhaps, new chances, one more chance –   260
Four great walls in the New Jerusalem
Meted on each side by the angel's reed,
For Leonard, Rafael, Agnolo and me
To cover – the three first without a wife,
While I have mine! So – still they overcome
Because there's still Lucrezia, – as I choose.

Again the Cousin's whistle! Go, my Love.

Robert Browning

To His Coy Mistress

Had we but world enough, and time,
This coyness, Lady, were no crime.
We would sit down, and think which way
To walk, and pass our long love's day.
Thou by the Indian Ganges' side
Shouldst rubies find: I by the tide
Of Humber would complain. I would
Love you ten years before the flood:
And you should, if you please, refuse
Till the conversion of the Jews.   10
My vegetable love should grow
Vaster than empires, and more slow.
An hundred years should go to praise
Thine eyes, and on thy forehead gaze.
Two hundred to adore each breast:
But thirty thousand to the rest.
An age at least to every part,
And the last age should show your heart:

For, Lady, you deserve this state;
Nor would I love at lower rate.   20
   But at my back I always hear
Time's wingèd chariot hurrying near:
And yonder all before us lie
Deserts of vast eternity.
Thy beauty shall no more be found;
Nor, in thy marble vault, shall sound
My echoing song: then worms shall try
That long-preserved virginity:
And your quaint honour turn to dust;
And into ashes all my lust.   30
The grave's a fine and private place,
But none, I think do there embrace.
   Now, therefore, while the youthful hew
Sits on thy skin like morning dew,
And while thy willing soul transpires
At every pore with instant fires,
Now let us sport us while we may;
And now, like amorous birds of prey,
Rather at once our time devour,
Than languish in his slow-chapped power.   40
Let us roll all our strength, and all
Our sweetness, up into one ball:
And tear our pleasures with rough strife,
Thorough the iron grates of life.
Thus, though we cannot make our sun
Stand still, yet we will make him run.

                                Andrew Marvell

One Flesh

Lying apart now, each in a separate bed,
He with a book, keeping the light on late,
She like a girl dreaming of childhood,
All men elsewhere – it is as if they wait
Some new event: the book he holds unread,
Her eyes fixed on the shadows overhead.

Tossed up like flotsam from a former passion,
How cool they lie. They hardly ever touch,
Or if they do it is like a confession
Of having little feeling – or too much.
Chastity faces them, a destination
For which their whole lives were a preparation.

Strangely apart, yet strangely close together,
Silence between them like a thread to hold
And not wind in. And time itself's a feather
Touching them gently. Do they know they're old,
These two who are my father and mother
Whose fire from which I came, has now grown cold?

Elizabeth Jennings

I Get a Kick Out of You

I get no kick from champagne;
Mere alcohol
Doesn't thrill me at all,
So tell me why should it be true
That I get a kick out of you.

Some get a kick from cocaine;
I'm sure that if
I took just one more sniff
That would bore me terrifically too.
Yet I get a kick out of you.

I get a kick every time I see you standing there before me –
I get a kick though it's patently clear that you obviously don't
　　adore me.

I get no kick in a plane;
Flying too high
With some bird in the sky
Is my idea of nothing to do.
Yet I get a kick out of you.

Cole Porter

Diary of a Church Mouse

Here among long-discarded cassocks,
Damp stools, and half-split open hassocks,
Here where the Vicar never looks
I nibble through old service books.
Lean and alone I spend my days
Behind this Church of England baize.
I share my dark forgotten room
With two oil-lamps and half a broom.
The cleaner never bothers me,
So here I eat my frugal tea.   10
My bread is sawdust mixed with straw;
My jam is polish for the floor.

Christmas and Easter may be feasts
For congregations and for priests,
And so may Whitsun. All the same,
They do not fill my meagre frame.
For me the only feast at all
Is Autumn's Harvest Festival,
When I can satisfy my want
With ears of corn around the font.   20
I climb the eagle's brazen head
To burrow through a loaf of bread.
I scramble up the pulpit stair
And gnaw the marrows hanging there.

It is enjoyable to taste
These items ere they go to waste,
But how annoying when one finds
That other mice with pagan minds
Come into church my food to share
Who have no proper business there.   30
Two field mice who have no desire
To be baptized, invade the choir.
A large and most unfriendly rat
Comes in to see what we are at.
He says he thinks there is no God
And yet he comes...it's rather odd.
This year he stole a sheaf of wheat
(It screened our special preacher's seat),
And prosperous mice from fields away

Come in to hear the organ play,   40
And under cover of its notes
Ate through the altar's sheaf of oats.
A Low Church mouse, who thinks that I
Am too papistical, and High,
Yet somehow doesn't think it wrong
To munch through Harvest Evensong,
While I, who starve the whole year through,
Must share my food with rodents who
Except at this time of the year
Not once inside the church appear.   50
    Within the human world I know
Such goings-on could not be so,
For human beings only do
What their religion tells them to.
They read the Bible every day
And always, night and morning, pray,
And just like me, the good church mouse,
Worship each week in God's own house.
    But all the same it's strange to me
How very full the church can be   60
With people I don't see at all
Except at Harvest Festival.

John Betjeman

Stopping by Woods on a Snowy Evening

Whose woods these are I think I know.
His house is in the village, though;
He will not see me stopping here
To watch his woods fill up with snow.

My little horse must think it queer
To stop without a farmhouse near
Between the woods and frozen lake
The darkest evening of the year.

He gives his harness bells a shake
To ask if there is some mistake.
The only other sound's the sweep
Of easy wind and downy flake.

The woods are lovely, dark, and deep,
But I have promises to keep,
And miles to go before I sleep,
And miles to go before I sleep.

Robert Frost

Soldiers Bathing

The sea at evening moves across the sand.
Under a reddening sky I watch the freedom of a band
Of soldiers who belong to me. Stripped bare
For bathing in the sea, they shout and run in the warm air;
Their flesh worn by the trade of war, revives
And my mind towards the meaning of it strives.

All's pathos now. The body that was gross,
Rank, ravenous, disgusting in the act or in repose,
All fever, filth and sweat, its bestial strength
And bestial decay, by pain and labour grows at length   10
Fragile and luminous. 'Poor bare forked animal',
Conscious of his desires and needs and flesh that rise and fall,
Stands in the soft air, tasting after toil
The sweetness of his nakedness: letting the sea-waves coil
Their frothy tongues about his feet, forgets
His hatred of the war, its terrible pressure that begets
A machinery of death and slavery,
Each being a slave and making slaves of others; finds that he
Remembers his old freedom in a game,
Mocking himself, and comically mimics fear and shame.   20

He plays with death and animality;
And reading in the shadows of his pallid flesh, I see
The idea of Michelangelo's cartoon
Of soldiers bathing, breaking off before they were half done
At some sortie of the enemy, an episode
Of the Pisan wars with Florence. I remember how he showed
Their muscular limbs that clamber from the water,
And heads that turn across the shoulder, eager for the
    slaughter,
Forgetful of their bodies that are bare,
And hot to buckle on and use the weapons lying there.   30
– And I think too of the theme another found
When, shadowing men's bodies on a sinister red ground,
Another Florentine, Pollaiuolo,
Painted a naked battle: warriors straddled, hacked the foe,
Dug their bare toes into the ground and slew
The brother-naked man who lay between their feet and drew
His lips back from his teeth in a grimace.

They were Italians who knew war's sorrow and disgrace
And showed the thing suspended, stripped – a theme
Born out of the experience of war's horrible extreme   40
Beneath a sky where even the air flows
With *lacrimae Christi*. For that rage, that bitterness, those blows,
That hatred of the slain, what could they be
But indirectly or directly a commentary
On the Crucifixion? And the picture burns
With indignation and pity and despair by turns,
Because it is the obverse of the scene
Where Christ hangs murdered, stripped, upon the Cross. I mean,
That is the explanation of its rage.

And we too have our bitterness and pity that engage   50
Blood, spirit in this war. But night begins,
Night of the mind: who nowadays is conscious of our sins?
Though every human deed concerns our blood,
And even we must know, what nobody has understood,
That some great love is over all we do,
And that is what has driven us to this fury, for so few
Can suffer all the terror of that love;
The terror of that love has set us spinning in this groove
Greased with our blood.   60
                    These dry themselves and dress,
Combing their hair, forget the fear and shame of nakedness.
Because to love is frightening we prefer
The freedom of our crimes. Yet, as I drink the dusky air,
I feel a strange delight that fills me full,
Strange gratitude, as if evil itself were beautiful;
And kiss the wound in thought, while in the west
I watch a streak of red that might have issued from Christ's
    breast.

F. T. Prince

EXAMINATIONS WITH AN 'OPEN BOOK'

There are some examination syllabuses which allow candidates to take texts they have studied into the examination. They are called open book syllabuses. The texts are 'plain', meaning that they do not have notes written in them.

The method of approach for these is similar to that for essays done in class. Keeping to the point of the question and demonstrating an awareness of relevant features of the language are the most important requirements.

These are also the most important requirements for dealing with previously unseen poems. In writing about poems which you might not have seen before, the basic principle is always to ask yourself why the particular words or expressions of the poem have been chosen. What advantage do they have in terms of:

(a) suggestions of meaning
(b) connections or associations with other words
(c) effects on other words close to them
(d) effects on rhythm, or on the pace of the poem
(e) images evoked
(f) sounds of the words
(g) creation of mood

It is worth looking at these one at a time in connection with the following poem:

Over the land freckled with snow half-thawed
The speculating rooks at their nests cawed
And saw from elm-tops, delicate as flower of grass,
What we below could not see, Winter pass.   *Edward Thomas*

(a) Suggestions of meaning
The word 'freckled' invites immediate attention because it is an unusual way of describing land. Freckles we associate with people's skin. In what way is 'freckled' different in suggestion, then, from spotted or blotched? The word 'speculating' is equally unusual. In what way can rooks be said to speculate? What do people do when they speculate? Why does this seem an appropriate word to use about the rooks in this context?

(b) Connections or associations with other words
Are there any other words which are suggested by the word speculate

through either their sound or their spelling? Are any of them appropriate here because they suggest ideas related to what the poem is saying?

(c) Effects on other words close to them

The effect one word can have on another which is close to it is to give it more impact through either emphasis or contrast. The word 'juxtaposition' means placing together or side by side. In the Edward Thomas poem you can see that the placing of 'saw' and 'cawed' has an effect in terms of rhyme, and the association of 'saw' with the sound the rooks make gives the word a more active function than it would have if it came, say, in the last line. The cawing of the rooks is meant to be the sound image which reverberates in the poem.

(d) Effects on rhythm, or the pace of the poem

Sometimes the punctuation determines the rhythm or pacing of the poem. What, for example, is the effect of the commas in the third line? Does the comma in the last line operate in the same way? Does the verse gain anything from this pause before the final two words?

Sometimes it is the pattern of stressed and unstressed syllables which determines the rhythm. In the phrase 'delicate as flower of grass' which are the three stressed syllables? Would the poem be any different if it were the third syllable of delicate which was stressed?

Sometimes it is the juxtaposition of consonants which affects the rhythm. Notice how the consonants in 'land freckled' have to be carefully negotiated. The same is true of 'nests cawed'.

(e) Images evoked

What image is evoked by calling the elm-tops 'delicate as flower of grass'? How does it help what is being said in the poem, to evoke this image? Is there a connection between the image in the first line and the final two words of the poem?

(f) Sounds of the words

The sounds of the words of this short poem have already been discussed in (c) and (d) above. But sometimes the special effect of sounds is not part of rhythm or a feature of juxtaposition. This is especially the case where the sound of the word reflects the sense of what it is describing – an effect known as onomatopoeia. The word 'cawed' is the most obvious example of this in the above poem.

(g) Creation of mood

How would you describe the mood of the poet in the poem above? Is his mood the same as that of the rooks he describes? The contrast between the two is another element in the poem's appeal.

164

'I have heard the mermaids singing'

My Busconductor

My busconductor tells me
he only has one kidney
and that may soon go on strike
through overwork.
Each busticket
takes on now a different shape
and texture.
He holds a ninepenny single
as if it were a rose
and puts the shilling in his bag   10
as a child into a gasmeter.
His thin lips
have no quips
for fat factorygirls
and he ignores
the drunk who snores
and the oldman who talks to himself
and gets off at the wrong stop.
He goes gently to the bedroom
of the bus   20
to collect
and watch familiar shops and pubs passby
(perhaps for the last time?)
The sameold streets look different now
more distinct
as through new glasses.
And the sky
was it ever so blue?

And all the time
deepdown in the deserted busshelter of his mind   30
he thinks about his journey nearly done.
One day he'll clock on and never clock off
or clock off and never clock on.   *Roger McGough*

The Second Coming

Turning and turning in the widening gyre
The falcon cannot hear the falconer;

Things fall apart; the centre cannot hold;
Mere anarchy is loosed upon the world,
The blood-dimmed tide is loosed, and everywhere
The ceremony of innocence is drowned;
The best lack all conviction, while the worst
Are full of passionate intensity.

Surely some revelation is at hand;
Surely the Second Coming is at hand.   10
The Second Coming! Hardly are those words out
When a vast image out of *Spiritus Mundi*
Troubles my sight: somewhere in sands of the desert
A shape with lion body and the head of a man,
A gaze blank and pitiless as the sun,
Is moving its slow thighs, while all about it
Reel shadows of the indignant desert birds.
The darkness drops again; but now I know
That twenty centuries of stony sleep
Were vexed to nightmare by a rocking cradle,   20
And what rough beast, its hour come round at last,
Slouches towards Bethlehem to be born?

W. B. Yeats

A Glass of Beer

The lanky hank of a she in the inn over there
Nearly killed me for asking the loan of a glass of beer;
May the devil grip the whey-faced slut by the hair,
And beat bad manners out of her skin for a year.

That parboiled ape, with the toughest jaw you will see
On virtue's path, and a voice that would rasp the dead,
Came roaring and raging the minute she looked at me;
And threw me out of the house on the back of my head!

If I asked her master he'd give me a cask a day;
But she, with the beer at hand, not a gill would arrange!
May she marry a ghost and bear him a kitten, and may
The High King of Glory permit her to get the mange.

James Stephens

Tom

Under the burnt out green
of this small yard's
tufts of grass
where water was once used
to wash pots, pans, poes,
ochre appears. A rusted
bucket, hole kicked into its
bottom, lies on its side.
Fence, low wall of careful
stones marking the square   10
yard, is broken now, breached
by pigs, by rats, by mongoose
and by neighbours. Eucalyptus
bushes push their way amidst
the marl. All looks so left
so unlived in: yard, fence and cabin.

Here old Tom lived: his whole
tight house no bigger than your
sitting room. Here was his world
banged like a fist on broken   20
chairs, bare table and the side-
board dresser where he kept his cups.
One wooden only door, still latched,
hasp broken; one window, wooden,
broken; four slats still intact.
Darkness pours from these wrecked boards
and from the crab-torn spaces underneath the door.

There are the deepest reaches of time's long
attack. The roof, dark shingles,
silvered in some places by the wind, the finger-   30
tips of weather, shines still secure, still
perfect, although the plaster peels from walls,
at sides, at back, from high up near the roof: in places
where it was not painted. But from the front,
the face from which it looked out on the world,
the house retains its lemon wash as smooth and bland as pearl.

But the tide creeps in: today's
insistence laps the loneliness of this
resisting cabin: the village grows and bulges:
shops, super-   40
market, Postal Agency
whose steel-spectacled mistress
rules the town. But no one knows
where Tom's cracked limestone oblong lies.
The house, the Postal Agent says,
is soon to be demolished:
a Housing Estate's being spawned
to feed the greedy town.

No one
knows Tom now, no one cares.   50
Slave's days are past, for-
gotten. The faith, the dream denied,
the things he dared
not do, all lost, if un-
forgiven. This house is all
that's left of hopes, of hurt,
of history...   *Edward Kamau Brathwaite*

The Love Song of J. Alfred Prufrock

S'io credesse che mia risposta fosse
A persona che mai tornasse al mondo,
Questa fiamma staria senza più scosse.
Ma per ciò che giammai di questo fondo
Non tornò viva alcun, s'i'odo il vero,
Senza tema d'infamia ti rispondo.

Let us go then, you and I,
When the evening is spread out against the sky
Like a patient etherised upon a table;
Let us go, through certain half-deserted streets,
The muttering retreats
Of restless nights in one-night cheap hotels
And sawdust restaurants with oyster-shells:
Streets that follow like a tedious argument
Of insidious intent
To lead you to an overwhelming question...   10
Oh, do not ask, 'What is it?'
Let us go and make our visit.

   In the room the women come and go
Talking of Michelangelo.

   The yellow fog that rubs its back upon the window-panes,
The yellow smoke that rubs its muzzle on the window-panes
Licked its tongue into the corners of the evening,
Lingered upon the pools that stand in drains,
Let fall upon its back the soot that falls from chimneys,
Slipped by the terrace, made a sudden leap,   20
And seeing that it was a soft October night,
Curled once about the house, and fell asleep.

   And indeed there will be time
For the yellow smoke that slides along the street
Rubbing its back upon the window-panes;
There will be time, there will be time
To prepare a face to meet the faces that you meet;
There will be time to murder and create,
And time for all the works and days of hands
That lift and drop a question on your plate;   30
Time for you and time for me,

169

And time yet for a hundred indecisions,
And for a hundred visions and revisions,
Before the taking of a toast and tea.

In the room the women come and go
Talking of Michelangelo.

And indeed there will be time
To wonder, 'Do I dare?' and, 'Do I dare?'
Time to turn back and descend the stair,
With a bald spot in the middle of my hair –   40
[They will say: 'How his hair is growing thin!']
My morning coat, my collar mounting firmly to the chin,
My necktie rich and modest, but asserted by a simple pin –
[They will say: 'But how his arms and legs are thin!']
Do I dare
Disturb the universe?
In a minute there is time
For decisions and revisions which a minute will reverse.

For I have known them all already, known them all –
Have known the evenings, mornings, afternoons,   50
I have measured out my life with coffee spoons;
I know the voices dying with a dying fall
Beneath the music from a farther room.
    So how should I presume?

And I have known the eyes already, known them all –
The eyes that fix you in a formulated phrase,
And when I am formulated, sprawling on a pin,
When I am pinned and wriggling on the wall,
Then how should I begin
To spit out all the butt-ends of my days and ways?   60
    And how should I presume?

And I have known the arms already, known them all –
Arms that are braceleted and white and bare
[But in the lamplight, downed with light brown hair!]
Is it perfume from a dress
That makes me so digress?

Arms that lie along a table, or wrap about a shawl.
And should I then presume?
And how should I begin?

      * * *

Shall I say, I have gone at dusk through narrow streets   70
And watched the smoke that rises from the pipes
Of lonely men in shirt-sleeves, leaning out of windows?...
    I should have been a pair of ragged claws
Scuttling across the floors of silent seas.

      * * *

And the afternoon, the evening, sleeps so peacefully!
Smoothed by long fingers,
Asleep...tired...or it malingers,
Stretched on the floor, here beside you and me.
Should I, after tea and cakes and ices,
Have the strength to force the moment to its crisis?   80
But though I have wept and fasted, wept and prayed,
Though I have seen my head [grown slightly bald] brought in
    upon a platter,
I am no prophet – and here's no great matter;
I have seen the moment of my greatness flicker,
And I have seen the eternal Footman hold my coat, and snicker,
And in short, I was afraid.

    And would it have been worth it, after all,
After the cups, the marmalade, the tea,
Among the porcelain, among some talk of you and me,
Would it have been worth while,   90
To have bitten off the matter with a smile,
To have squeezed the universe into a ball
To roll it toward some overwhelming question,
To say: 'I am Lazarus, come from the dead,
Come back to tell you all, I shall tell you all' –
If one, settling a pillow by her head,
    Should say: 'That is not what I meant at all.
    That is not it, at all.'

And would it have been worth it, after all,
Would it have been worth while,   100
After the sunsets and the dooryards and the sprinkled streets,
After the novels, after the teacups, after the skirts that trail
    along the floor –
And this, and so much more? –
It is impossible to say just what I mean!
But as if a magic lantern threw the nerves in patterns on a
    screen:
Would it have been worth while
If one, settling a pillow or throwing off a shawl,
And turning toward the window, should say:
    'That is not it at all,
    That is not what I meant, at all.'   110

        *   *   *

No! I am not Prince Hamlet, nor was meant to be;
Am an attendant lord, one that will do
To swell a progress, start a scene or two,
Advise the prince; no doubt, an easy tool,
Deferential, glad to be of use,
Politic, cautious, and meticulous;
Full of high sentence, but a bit obtuse;
At times, indeed, almost ridiculous –
Almost, at times, the Fool.

    I grow old...I grow old...   120
I shall wear the bottoms of my trousers rolled.

    Shall I part my hair behind? Do I dare to eat a peach?
I shall wear white flannel trousers, and walk upon the beach.
I have heard the mermaids singing, each to each.

    I do not think that they will sing to me.

    I have seen them riding seaward on the waves
Combing the white hair of the wave blown back
When the wind blows the water white and black.

We have lingered in the chambers of the sea
By sea-girls wreathed with seaweed red and brown   130
Till human voices wake us, and we drown.

T. S. Eliot

Menelaus and Helen

I

Hot through Troy's ruin Menelaus broke
  To Priam's palace, sword in hand, to sate
  On that adulterous whore a ten years' hate
And a king's honour. Through red death, and smoke,
And cries, and then by quieter ways he strode,
  Till the still innermost chamber fronted him.
  He swung his sword, and crashed into the dim
Luxurious bower, flaming like a god.

High sat white Helen, lonely and serene.
  He had not remembered that she was so fair,   10
And that her neck curved down in such a way;
  And he felt tired. He flung the sword away,
  And kissed her feet, and knelt before her there,
The perfect Knight before the perfect Queen.

II

So far the poet. How should he behold
  That journey home, the long connubial years?
  He does not tell you how white Helen bears
Child on legitimate child, becomes a scold,
Haggard with virtue. Menelaus bold
  Waxed garrulous, and sacked a hundred Troys   20
  'Twixt noon and supper. And her golden voice
Got shrill as he grew deafer. And both were old.

Often he wonders why on earth he went
  Troyward, or why poor Paris ever came.
Oft she weeps, gummy-eyed and impotent;
  Her dry shanks twitch at Paris' mumbled name.
So Menelaus nagged; and Helen cried;
And Paris slept on by Scamander side.

Rupert Brooke

The Hunchback in the Park

The hunchback in the park
A solitary mister
Propped between trees and water
From the opening of the garden lock
That lets the trees and water enter
Until the Sunday sombre bell at dark

Eating bread from a newspaper
Drinking water from the chained cup
That the children filled with gravel
In the fountain basin where I sailed my ship   10
Slept at night in a dog kennel
But nobody chained him up.

Like the park birds he came early
Like the water he sat down
And Mister they called Hey mister
The truant boys from the town
Running when he had heard them clearly
On out of sound

Past lake and rockery
Laughing when he shook his paper   20
Hunchbacked in mockery
Through the loud zoo of the willow groves
Dodging the park keeper
With his stick that picked up leaves.

And the old dog sleeper
Alone between nurses and swans
While the boys among willows
Made the tigers jump out of their eyes
To roar on the rockery stones
And the groves were blue with sailors   30

Made all day until bell time
A woman figure without fault
Straight as a young elm
Straight and tall from his crooked bones
That she might stand in the night
After the locks and chains

174

All night in the unmade park
After the railings and shrubberies
The birds the grass the trees the lake
And the wild boys innocent as strawberries   40
Had followed the hunchback
To his kennel in the dark.

Dylan Thomas

Death on a Live Wire

Treading a field I saw afar
A laughing fellow climbing the cage
That held the grinning tensions of wire,
Alone, and no girl gave him courage.

Up he climbed on the diamond struts,
Diamond cut diamond, till he stood
With the insulators brooding like owls
And all their live wisdom, if he would.

I called to him climbing and asked him to say
What thrust him into the singeing sky: 10
The one word he told me the wind took away,
So I shouted again, but the wind passed me by

And the gust of his answer tore at his coat
And struck him stark on the lightning's bough;
Humanity screeched in his manacled throat
And he cracked with flame like a figure of straw.

Turning, burning, he dangled black,
A hot sun swallowing at his fork
And shaking embers out of his back,
Planting his shadow of fear in the chalk.   20

O then he danced an incredible dance
With soot in his sockets, hanging at heels:
Uprooted mandrakes screamed in his loins,
His legs thrashed and lashed like electric eels;

175

Reposition

For now he embraced the talent of iron,
The white-hot ore that comes from the hill,
The Word out of which the electrons run,
The snake in the rod and the miracle;
And as he embraced it the girders turned black,
Fused metal wept and great tears ran down,   30
Till his fingers like snails at last came unstuck
And he fell through the cage of the sun.

                                        Michael Baldwin

Pain

All was quiet in this park
Until the wind, like a gasping messenger, announced
The tyrant's coming.
Then did the branches talk in agony.

You remember that raging storm?

In their fear despairing flowers nevertheless held bouquets to the
    grim king;

Meteors were the tassels of his crown
While like branches that only spoke when the storm menaced
We cried in agony as we fell
Slashed by the cold blade of an invisible sword.

Mutilated our limbs were swept away by the rain
But not our blood;
Indelible, it stuck on the walls
Like wild gum on tree-trunks.

                                        Mbella Sonne Dipoko

The Lotos-Eaters

'Courage!' he said, and pointed toward the land,
'This mounting wave will roll us shoreward soon.'
In the afternoon they came unto a land,
In which it seemed always afternoon.
All round the coast the languid air did swoon,
Breathing like one that hath a weary dream.
Full-faced above the valley stood the moon;
And like a downward smoke, the slender stream
Along the cliff to fall and pause and fall did seem.

A land of streams! some, like a downward smoke,   10
Slow-dropping veils of thinnest lawn, did go;
And some thro' wavering lights and shadows broke,
Rolling a slumbrous sheet of foam below.
They saw the gleaming river seaward flow
From the inner land: far off, three mountain-tops,
Three silent pinnacles of aged snow,
Stood sunset-flush'd: and, dew'd with showery drops,
Up-clomb the shadowy pine above the woven copse.

The charmed sunset linger'd low adown
In the red West: thro' mountain clefts the dale   20
Was seen far inland, and the yellow down
Border'd with palm, and many a winding vale
And meadow, set with slender galingale;
A land where all things always seem'd the same!
And round about the keel with faces pale,
Dark faces pale against that rosy flame,
The mild-eyed melancholy Lotos-eaters came.

Branches they bore of that enchanted stem,
Laden with flower and fruit, whereof they gave
To each, but whoso did receive of them,   30
And taste, to him the gushing of the wave
Far far away did seem to mourn and rave
On alien shores; and if his fellow spake,
His voice was thin, as voices from the grave;
And deep-asleep he seem'd, yet all awake,
And music in his ears his beating heart did make.

They sat them down upon the yellow sand,
Between the sun and moon upon the shore;
And sweet it was to dream of Father-land,
Of child, and wife, and slave; but evermore   40
Most weary seem'd the sea, weary the oar,
Weary the wandering fields of barren foam.
Then some one said, 'We will return no more';
And all at once they sang, 'Our island home
Is far beyond the wave; we will no longer roam.'

CHORIC SONG

I

There is sweet music here that softer falls
Than petals from blown roses on the grass,
Or night-dews on still waters between walls
Of shadowy granite, in a gleaming pass;
Music that gentlier on the spirit lies,   50
Than tir'd eyelids upon tir'd eyes;
Music that brings sweet sleep down from the blissful skies.
Here are cool mosses deep,
And thro' the moss the ivies creep,
And in the stream the long-leaved flowers weep,
And from the craggy ledge the poppy hangs in sleep.

II

Why are we weigh'd upon with heaviness,
And utterly consumed with sharp distress,
While all things else have rest from weariness?
All things have rest: why should we toil alone,   60
We only toil, who are the first of things,
And make perpetual moan,
Still from one sorrow to another thrown:
Nor ever fold our wings,
And cease from wanderings,
Nor steep our brows in slumber's holy balm;
Nor harken what the inner spirit sings,
'There is no joy but calm!'
Why should we only toil, the roof and crown of things?

III

Lo! in the middle of the wood,   70
The folded leaf is woo'd from out the bud
With winds upon the branch, and there
Grows green and broad, and takes no care,
Sun-steep'd at noon, and in the moon
Nightly dew-fed; and turning yellow
Falls, and floats adown the air.
Lo! sweeten'd with the summer light,
The full-juiced apple, waxing over-mellow,
Drops in a silent autumn night.
All its allotted length of days,   80
The flower ripens in its place,
Ripens and fades, and falls, and hath no toil,
Fast-rooted in the fruitful soil.

IV

Hateful is the dark-blue sky
Vaulted o'er the dark-blue sea.
Death is the end of life; ah, why
Should life all labour be?
Let us alone. Time driveth onward fast,
And in a little while our lips are dumb.
Let us alone. What is it that will last?   90
All things are taken from us, and become
Portions and parcels of the dreadful Past.
Let us alone. What pleasure can we have
To war with evil? Is there any peace
In ever climbing up the climbing wave?
All things have rest, and ripen toward the grave
In silence; ripen, fall and cease:
Give us long rest or death, dark death, or dreamful ease.

V

How sweet it were, hearing the downward stream,
With half-shut eyes ever to seem   100
Falling asleep in a half-dream!
To dream and dream, like yonder amber light,
Which will not leave the myrrh-bush on the height;
To hear each other's whisper'd speech;
Eating the Lotos day by day,

To watch the crisping ripples on the beach,
And tender curving lines of creamy spray;
To lend our hearts and spirits wholly
To the influence of mild-minded melancholy;
To muse and brood and live again in memory, 110
With those old faces of our infancy
Heap'd over with a mound of grass,
Two handfuls of white dust, shut in an urn of brass!

VI

Dear is the memory of our wedded lives,
And dear the last embraces of our wives
And their warm tears: but all hath suffer'd change;
For surely now our household hearths are cold:
Our sons inherit us: our looks are strange:
And we should come like ghosts to trouble joy.
Or else the island princes over-bold 120
Have eat our substance, and the minstrel sings
Before them of the ten years' war in Troy,
And our great deeds, as half-forgotten things.
Is there confusion in the little isle?
Let what is broken so remain.
The Gods are hard to reconcile:
'Tis hard to settle order once again.
There *is* confusion worse than death,
Trouble on trouble, pain on pain,
Long labour unto aged breath, 130
Sore task to hearts worn out with many wars
And eyes grown dim with gazing on the pilot-stars.

VII

But, propt on beds of amaranth and moly,
How sweet (while warm airs lull us, blowing lowly)
With half-dropt eyelid still,
Beneath a heaven dark and holy
To watch the long bright river drawing slowly
His waters from the purple hill –
To hear the dewy echoes calling
From cave to cave thro' the thick-twined vine – 140
To watch the emerald-colour'd water falling
Thro' many a wov'n acanthus-wreath divine!
Only to hear and see the far-off sparkling brine,
Only to hear were sweet, stretch'd out beneath the pine.

The Lotos blooms below the barren peak:
The Lotos blows by every winding creek:
All day the wind breathes low with mellower tone:
Thro' every hollow cave and alley lone
Round and round the spicy downs the yellow Lotos-dust is
    blown.
We have had enough of action, and of motion we,   150
Roll'd to starboard, roll'd to larboard, when the surge was
    seething free,
Where the wallowing monster spouted his foam-fountains in the
    sea.
Let us swear an oath, and keep it with an equal mind,
In the hollow Lotos-land to live and lie reclined
On the hills like Gods together, careless of mankind.
For they lie beside their nectar, and the bolts are hurl'd
Far below them in the valleys, and the clouds are lightly curl'd
Round their golden houses, girdled with the gleaming world:
Where they smile in secret, looking over wasted lands,
Blight and famine, plague and earthquake, roaring deeps and   160
    fiery sands,
Clanging fights, and flaming towns, and sinking ships, and
    praying hands.
But they smile, they find a music centred in a doleful song
Steaming up, a lamentation and an ancient tale of wrong,
Like a tale of little meaning tho' the words are strong;
Chanted from an ill-used race of men that cleave the soil,
Sow the seed, and reap the harvest with enduring toil,
Storing yearly little dues of wheat, and wine and oil;
Till they perish and they suffer – some, 'tis whisper'd – down in
    hell
Suffer endless anguish, others in Elysian valleys dwell,
Resting weary limbs at last on beds of asphodel.   170
Surely, surely, slumber is more sweet than toil, the shore
Than labour in the deep mid-ocean, wind and wave and oar;
Oh rest ye, brother mariners, we will not wander more.

Alfred, Lord Tennyson

Macaw and Little Miss

In a cage of wire-ribs
The size of a man's head, the macaw bristles in a staring
Combustion, suffers the stoking devils of his eyes.
In the old lady's parlour, where an aspidistra succumbs
To the musk of faded velvet, he hangs as in clear flames,
   Like a torturer's iron instrument preparing
   With dense slow shudderings of greens, yellows, blues,
      Crimsoning into the barbs:

Or like the smouldering head that hung
In Killdevil's brass kitchen, in irons, who had been   10
Volcano swearing to vomit the world away in black ash,
And would, one day; or a fugitive aristocrat
From some thunderous mythological hierarchy, caught
   By a little boy with a crust and a bent pin,
   Or snare of horsehair set for a song-thrush,
      And put in a cage to sing.

The old lady who feeds him seeds
Has a grand-daughter. The girl calls him 'Poor Polly', pokes fun.
'Jolly Mop.' But lies under every full moon,
The spun glass of her body bared and so gleam-still   20
Her brimming eyes do not tremble or spill
   The dream where the warrior comes, lightning and iron,
   Smashing and burning and rending towards her loin:
      Deep into her pillow her silence pleads.

All day he stares at his furnace
With eyes red-raw, but when she comes they close.
'Polly. Pretty Poll', she cajoles, and rocks him gently.
She caresses, whispers kisses. The blue lids stay shut.
She strikes the cage in a tantrum and swirls out:
   Instantly beak, wings, talons crash   30
   The bars in conflagration and frenzy,
      And his shriek shakes the house.

                   Ted Hughes

Digging

Between my finger and my thumb
The squat pen rests; snug as a gun.

Under my window, a clean rasping sound
When the spade sinks into gravelly ground:
My father, digging. I look down

Till his straining rump among the flowerbeds
Bends low, comes up twenty years away
Stooping in rhythm through potato drills
Where he was digging.

The coarse boot nestled on the lug, the shaft   10
Against the inside knee was levered firmly.
He rooted out tall tops, buried the bright edge deep
To scatter new potatoes that we picked
Loving their cool hardness in our hands.

By God, the old man could handle a spade.
Just like his old man.

My grandfather cut more turf in a day
Than any other man on Toner's bog.
Once I carried him milk in a bottle
Corked sloppily with paper. He straightened up   20
To drink it, then fell to right away
Nicking and slicing neatly, heaving sods
Over his shoulder, going down and down
For the good turf. Digging.

The cold smell of potato mould, the squelch and slap
Of soggy peat, the curt cuts of an edge
Through living roots awaken in my head.
But I've no spade to follow men like them.

Between my finger and my thumb
The squat pen rests.   30
I'll dig with it.

Seamus Heaney

Swedes

They have taken the gable from the roof of clay
On the long swede pile. They have let in the sun
To the white and gold and purple of curled fronds
Unsunned. It is a sight more tender-gorgeous
At the wood-corner where Winter moans and drips
Than when, in the Valley of the Tombs of Kings,
A boy crawls down into a Pharaoh's tomb
And, first of Christian men, beholds the mummy,
God and monkey, chariot and throne and vase,
Blue pottery, alabaster, and gold.

But dreamless long-dead Amen-hotep lies.
This is a dream of Winter, sweet as Spring.

Edward Thomas

The Ecstatic

Lark, skylark, spilling your rubbed and round
Pebbles of sound in air's still lake,
Whose widening circles fill the noon; yet none
Is known so small beside the sun:

Be strong your fervent soaring, your skyward air!
Tremble there, a nerve of song!
Float up there where voice and wing are one,
A singing star, a note of light!

Buoyed, embayed in heaven's noon-wide reaches –
For soon light's tide will turn – oh stay!
Cease not till day streams to the west, then down
That estuary drop down to peace.

C. Day Lewis

The Good Morrow

I wonder by my troth, what thou, and I
    Did, till we lov'd? were we not wean'd till then?
But suck'd on countrey pleasures, childishly?
    Or snorted we in the seaven sleepers den?
T'was so; But this, all pleasures fancies bee.
If ever any beauty I did see,
Which I desir'd, and got, t'was but a dreame of thee.

And now good morrow to our waking soules,
    Which watch not one another out of feare;
For love, all love of other sights controules,   10
    And makes one little roome, an every where.
Let sea-discoverers to new worlds have gone,
Let Maps to other, worlds on worlds have showne,
Let us possesse one world, each hath one, and is one.

My face in thine eye, thine in mine appeares,
    And true plaine hearts doe in the faces rest,
Where can we finde two better hemispheares
    Without sharpe North, without declining West?
What ever dyes, was not mixt equally;
If our two loves be one, or, thou and I   20
Love so alike, that none doe slacken, none can die.

John Donne

The Woodspurge

The wind flapped loose, the wind was still,
Shaken out dead from tree and hill:
I had walked on at the wind's will, –
I sat now, for the wind was still.

Between my knees my forehead was, –
My lips, drawn in, said not Alas!
My hair was over in the grass,
My naked ears heard the day pass.

My eyes, wide open, had the run
Of some ten weeds to fix upon;
Among those few, out of the sun,
The woodspurge flowered, three cups in one.

From perfect grief there need not be
Wisdom or even memory:
One thing then learnt remains to me, –
The woodspurge has a cup of three.

D. G. Rossetti

Toads

Why should I let the toad work
    Squat on my life?
Can't I use my wit as a pitchfork
    And drive the brute off?

Six days of the week it soils
    With its sickening poison –
Just for paying a few bills!
    That's out of proportion.

Lots of folk live on their wits:
    Lecturers, lispers,   10
Losels, loblolly-men, louts –
    They don't end as paupers;

Lots of folk live up lanes
    With fires in a bucket,
Eat windfalls and tinned sardines –
    They seem to like it.

Their nippers have got bare feet,
    Their unspeakable wives
Are skinny as whippets – and yet
    No one actually *starves*.   20

Ah, were I courageous enough
    To shout *Stuff your pension!*
But I know, all too well, that's the stuff
    That dreams are made on:

For something sufficiently toad-like
    Squats in me, too;
Its hunkers are heavy as hard luck,
    And cold as snow,

And will never allow me to blarney
    My way to getting   30
The fame and the girl and the money
    All at one sitting.

I don't say, one bodies the other
    One's spiritual truth;
But I *do say* it's hard to lose either,
    When you have both.

                Philip Larkin

Toads Revisited

Walking around in the park
Should feel better than work:
The lake, the sunshine,
The grass to lie on,

Blurred playground noises
Beyond black-stockinged nurses –
Not a bad place to be.
Yet it doesn't suit me,

Being one of the men
You meet of an afternoon: 10
Palsied old step-takers,
Hare-eyed clerks with the jitters,

Waxed-fleshed out-patients
Still vague from accidents,
And characters in long coats
Deep in the litter-baskets –

All dodging the toad work
By being stupid or weak.
Think of being them!
Hearing the hours chime,   20

Watching the bread delivered,
The sun by clouds covered,
The children going home;
Think of being them,

Turning over their failures
By some bed of lobelias,
Nowhere to go but indoors,
No friends but empty chairs –

No, give me my in-tray,
My loaf-haired secretary,   30
My shall-I-keep-the-call-in-Sir:
What else can I answer,

When the lights come on at four
At the end of another year?
Give me your arm, old toad;
Help me down Cemetery Road.

Philip Larkin

Ode to a Nightingale

My heart aches, and a drowsy numbness pains
    My sense, as though of hemlock I had drunk,
Or emptied some dull opiate to the drains
    One minute past, and Lethe-wards had sunk:
'Tis not through envy of thy happy lot,
    But being too happy in thine happiness, –
        That thou, light-winged Dryad of the trees,
            In some melodious plot
    Of beechen green, and shadows numberless,
        Singest of summer in full-throated ease.   10

O, for a draught of vintage! that hath been
    Cool'd a long age in the deep-delved earth,
Tasting of Flora and the country green,
    Dance, and Provençal song, and sunburnt mirth!
O for a beaker full of the warm South,
    Full of the true, the blushful Hippocrene,
        With beaded bubbles winking at the brim,
            And purple-stained mouth;
That I might drink, and leave the world unseen,
    And with thee fade away into the forest dim: 20

Fade far away, dissolve, and quite forget
What thou among the leaves hast never known,
The weariness, the fever, and the fret
Here, where men sit and hear each other groan;
Where palsy shakes a few, sad, last gray hairs,
Where youth grows pale, and spectre-thin, and dies;
Where but to think is to be full of sorrow
And leaden-eyed despairs,
Where Beauty cannot keep her lustrous eyes,
Or new Love pine at them beyond to-morrow.   30

Away! away! for I will fly to thee,
Not charioted by Bacchus and his pards,
But on the viewless wings of Poesy,
Though the dull brain perplexes and retards:
Already with thee! tender is the night,
And haply the Queen-Moon is on her throne,
Cluster'd around by all her starry Fays;
But here there is no light,
Save what from heaven is with the breezes blown
Through verdurous glooms and winding mossy ways.   40

I cannot see what flowers are at my feet,
Nor what soft incense hangs upon the boughs,
But, in embalmed darkness, guess each sweet
Wherewith the seasonable month endows
The grass, the thicket, and the fruit-tree wild;
White hawthorn, and the pastoral eglantine;
Fast fading violets cover'd up in leaves;
And mid-May's eldest child,
The coming musk-rose, full of dewy wine,
The murmurous haunt of flies on summer eves.   50

Darkling I listen; and, for many a time
  I have been half in love with easeful Death,
Call'd him soft names in many a mused rhyme,
  To take into the air my quiet breath;
Now more than ever seems it rich to die,
  To cease upon the midnight with no pain,
    While thou art pouring forth thy soul abroad
      In such an ecstasy!
    Still wouldst thou sing, and I have ears in vain –
      To thy high requiem become a sod.   60

Thou wast not born for death, immortal Bird!
  No hungry generations tread thee down;
The voice I hear this passing night was heard
  In ancient days by emperor and clown:
Perhaps the self-same song that found a path
  Through the sad heart of Ruth, when, sick for home,
    She stood in tears amid the alien corn;
      The same that oft-times hath
    Charm'd magic casements, opening on the foam
      Of perilous seas, in faery lands forlorn.   70

Forlorn! the very word is like a bell
  To toll me back from thee to my sole self!
Adieu! the fancy cannot cheat so well
  As she is fam'd to do, deceiving elf.
Adieu! adieu! thy plaintive anthem fades
  Past the near meadows, over the still stream,
    Up the hill-side; and now 'tis buried deep
      In the next valley-glades:
    Was it a vision, or a waking dream?
      Fled is that music: – Do I wake or sleep?   80

John Keats

Sonnet 18

Shall I compare thee to a Summer's day?
Thou art more lovely and more temperate:
Rough winds do shake the darling buds of May,
And Summer's lease hath all too short a date:
Sometime too hot the eye of heaven shines,
And often is his gold complexion dimm'd,
And every fair from fair sometime declines,
By chance, or nature's changing course untrimm'd:
But thy eternal Summer shall not fade,
Nor lose possession of that fair thou ow'st,
Nor shall Death brag thou wander'st in his shade,
When in eternal lines to time thou grow'st:
   So long as men can breathe or eyes can see,
   So long lives this, and this gives life to thee.

William Shakespeare

The Garden

1

How vainly men themselves amaze
To win the palm, the oak, or bays,
And their uncessant labours see
Crowned from some single herb or tree,
Whose short and narrow vergèd shade
Does prudently their toils upbraid,
While all flow'rs and all trees do close
To weave the garlands of repose.

2

Fair Quiet, have I found thee here,
And Innocence, thy sister dear?   10
Mistaken long, I sought you then
In busy companies of men.
Your sacred plants, if here below,
Only among the plants will grow.
Society is all but rude,
To this delicious solitude.

3

No white nor red was ever seen
So am'rous as this lovely green.
Fond lovers, cruel as their flame,
Cut in these trees their mistress' name.   20
Little, alas, they know, or heed,
How far these beauties hers exceed!
Fair trees! wheres'e'er your barks I wound,
No name shall but your own be found.

4

When we have run our passion's heat,
Love hither makes his best retreat.
The gods, that mortal beauty chase,
Still in a tree did end their race.
Apollo hunted Daphne so,
Only that she might laurel grow.   30
And Pan did after Syrinx speed,
Not as a nymph, but for a reed.

5

What wondrous life is this I lead!
Ripe apples drop about my head;
The luscious clusters of the vine
Upon my mouth do crush their wine;
The nectarene, and curious peach,
Into my hands themselves do reach;
Stumbling on melons, as I pass,
Ensnared with flowers, I fall on grass.   40

6

Meanwhile the mind, from pleasures less,
Withdraws into its happiness:
The mind, that ocean where each kind
Does straight its own resemblance find,
Yet it creates, transcending these,
Far other worlds, and other seas,
Annihilating all that's made
To a green thought in a green shade.

7

Here at the fountain's sliding foot,
Or at some fruit-tree's mossy root,   50
Casting the body's vest aside,
My soul into the boughs does glide:
There like a bird it sits, and sings,
Then whets, and combs its silver wings;
And, till prepared for longer flight,
Waves in its plumes the various light.

8

Such was that happy garden-state,
While man there walked without a mate:
After a place so pure, and sweet,
What other help could yet be meet!   60
But 'twas beyond a mortal's share
To wander solitary there:
Two paradises 'twere in one
To live in paradise alone.

9

How well the skilful gardener drew
Of flowers and herbs this dial new,
Where from above the milder sun
Does through a fragrant zodiac run;
And, as it works, the industrious bee
Computes its time as well as we.   70
How could such sweet and wholesome hours
Be reckoned but with herbs and flowers!

Andrew Marvell

Nicholson, Suddenly

From the *Barrow Evening Mail*, Thurs, 13 Feb., 1969.

'NICHOLSON – (Suddenly) on February 11, Norman, aged 57 years, beloved husband of Mona Nicholson, and dear father of Gerald, of 6 Atkinson Street, Haverigg, Millom.'

So Norman Nicholson is dead!
I saw him just three weeks ago
Standing outside a chemist's shop,
His smile alight, his cheeks aglow.
I'd never seen him looking finer:
'I can't complain at all,' he said,
'But for a touch of the old angina.'
Then hobbled in for his prescription.
Born in one town, we'd made our start,
Though not in any way related,   10
Two years and three streets apart,
Under one nominal description:
'Nicholson, Norman', entered, dated,
In registers of birth and school.
In 1925 we sat
At the same desk in the same class –
Me, chatty, natty, nervous, thin,
Quick for the turn of the teacher's chin;
Silent, shy and smiling, he,
And fleshed enough for two of me – 20
An unidentical near twin
Who never pushed his presence in
When he could keep it out.
      For seven
Years after that each neither knew,
Nor cared much, where or even whether
The other lived. And then, together,
We nearly booked out berths to heaven: –
Like a church weathercock, *I* crew
A graveyard cough and went to bed 30
For fifteen months; *he* dropped a lead
Pipe on his foot and broke them both.
They wheeled him home to his young wife
Half-crippled for the rest of life.

In three decades or more since then
We met, perhaps, two years in ten
In shops or waiting for a bus;
Greeted each other without fuss,
Just: 'How do, Norman?' – Didn't matter
Which of us spoke – we said the same.   40
And now and then we'd stop to natter:
'How's the leg?' or 'How's the chest?' –
He a crock below the waist
And me a crock above it.
                          Blessed
Both with a certain home-bred gumption,
We stumped our way across the cobbles
Of half a life-time's bumps and roughness –
He short in step and me in wind,
Yet with a kind of wiry toughness.   50
Each rather sorry for the other,
We chose the road that suited best –
Neither inscribed the sky with flame;
Neither disgraced the other's name.
And now, perhaps, one day a year
The town will seem for half a minute
A place with one less person in it,
When I remember I'll not meet
My unlike double in the street.
Postmen will mix us up no more,   60
Taking my letters to his door,
For which I ought to raise a cheer.
But can I stir myself to thank
My lucky stars, when there's a blank
Where his stars were? For I'm left here,
Wearing his name as well as mine,
Finding the new one doesn't fit,
And though I'll make the best of it,
Sad that such things had to be –
But glad, still, that it wasn't me.   70

Norman Nicholson

LEARNING POETRY BY HEART

Years ago the main element of teaching poetry in schools seemed to be getting the students to learn vast amounts of poetry by heart. Often students were required to be able to recite poetry without ever having its meaning explained to them; or indeed without being required to reflect upon the meaning of what they were learning. Consequently there was a fierce reaction to this pattern – an over-reaction, in fact – which resulted in the total abandonment of any close learning of poetry.

As it happens, most people who study or read poetry to an advanced level do know lots of poetry by heart. It helps them to discuss literary questions when they have what amounts to the raw material at their finger-tips – or stored in their minds for instant retrieval as the occasion demands.

Knowing poems well helps you to understand one of its most important effects – the effect of rhythm. It can seem very shoddy when a student produces in an essay a quotation which is so inaccurate that its rhythm is destroyed. This can be especially damaging if the essay is trying to explain the effects of the sound of the poem. After all, it must look totally unconvincing and insincere to extol the beauties of a piece of writing when the misquotation offered reveals in itself the student's lack of sensitivity to poetic effects.

Besides, part of the study of literature is based upon the sense of enjoyment derived from the subject. Enjoyment comes with commitment and familiarity. The lines students learn from poetry are often a source of genuine satisfaction since they constitute part of their cultural interest.

Like any other activity, it is best done when the choice is your own. And as with any other interest or hobby, you should not expect all your friends to be enthusiastic about your own tastes and knowledge. So don't be surprised if your friends do not want to listen to you reciting verse. Be content with your own achievement.

There are various approaches to learning poetry, but a method which has been found most effective is to read it into a tape recorder and play it back while reading the text. Some people find they can remember what they hear much more easily than what they read. This is why a tape recording can be a useful supplement to a printed book.

Lines of poetry can be learned more easily than lines of prose since both the rhythm and the number of syllables in the line are aids to

197

memory. So is the rhyme, of course, in rhyming verse. If the poetry is written in free verse, then it can be easier to learn it in sentences than in lines.

Another way of learning parts of poems is through the repeated use of key quotations when writing your practice essays. Certainly it can give you a lot of confidence in an examination to know that you can refer in considerable detail to some poems, at least. But always remember that however much you know of a poem, quote only the shortest amount possible to support any given point you are making.

During your course you will come across certain phrases or lines which seem so central to the ideas of a particular author that you find yourself using them in a variety of contexts. These often stick in your memory without any active attempt to learn them. These quotations can be invaluable.

Probably the best advice on learning poetry is to learn only that which you personally want to learn because it has some special appeal for you.

APPENDIX

The following poems by Gerard Manley Hopkins are referred to in the examples of essays written for examinations (pp. 69–72).

Inversnaid

This darksome burn, horseback brown,
His rollrock highroad roaring down,
In coop and in comb the fleece of his foam
Flutes and low to the lake falls home.

A windpuff-bonnet of fawn-froth
Turns and twindles over the broth
Of a pool so pitchblack, fell-frowning,
It rounds and rounds Despair to drowning.

Degged with dew, dappled with dew
Are the groins of the braes that the brook treads through,
Wiry heathpacks, flitches of fern,
And the beadbonny ash that sits over the burn.

What would the world be, once bereft
Of wet and wildness? Let them be left,
O let them be left, wildness and wet;
Long live the weeds and the wilderness yet.

Spring

Nothing is so beautiful as spring –
  When weeds, in wheels, shoot long and lovely and lush;
  Thrush's eggs look little low heavens, and thrush
Through the echoing timber does so rinse and wring
The ear, it strikes like lightnings to hear him sing;
  The glassy peartree leaves and blooms, they brush
  The descending blue; that blue is all in a rush

With richness; the racing lambs too have fair their fling.
What is all this juice and all this joy?
A strain of the earth's sweet being in the beginning
In Eden garden. – Have, get, before it cloy,
Before it cloud, Christ, lord, and sour with sinning,
Innocent mind and Mayday in girl and boy,
Most, O maid's child, thy choice and worthy the winning.

Binsey Poplars

felled 1879

My aspens dear, whose airy cages quelled,
Quelled or quenched in leaves the leaping sun,
All felled, felled, are all felled;
   Of a fresh and following folded rank
       Not spared, not one
       That dandled a sandalled
     Shadow that swam or sank
On meadow and river and wind-wandering weed-winding bank.

O if we but knew what we do
    When we delve or hew –   10
Hack and rack the growing green!
   Since country is so tender
To touch, her being so slender,
That, like this sleek and seeing ball
But a prick will make no eye at all,
Where we, even where we mean
     To mend her we end her,
   When we hew or delve:
After-comers cannot guess the beauty been.
   Ten or twelve, only ten or twelve   20
   Strokes of havoc unselve
     The sweet especial scene,
  Rural scene, a rural scene,
  Sweet especial rural scene.

Pied Beauty

Glory be to God for dappled things –
  For skies of couple-colour as a brinded cow;
    For rose-moles all in stipple upon trout that swim;
  Fresh-firecoal chestnut-falls; finches' wings;
  Landscape plotted and pieced – fold, fallow, and plough;
    And all trades, their gear and tackle and trim.

All things counter, original, spare, strange;
  Whatever is fickle, freckled (who knows how?)
    With swift, slow; sweet, sour; adazzle, dim;
He fathers-forth whose beauty is past change:
        Praise him.

INDEX OF FIRST LINES

THE POETS

(with date and place of birth, and date of death)

Chinua Achebe	1930 Ogidi, Nigeria	
Matthew Arnold	1822 Middlesex, England	1888
Wystan Hugh Auden	1907 York, England	1973
Michael Baldwin	1930 Kent, England	
John Betjeman	1906 London, England	1984
William Blake	1757 London, England	1827
Edward Kamau Brathwaite	1930 Barbados, West Indies	
Edwin Brock	1927 London, England	
Emily Brontë	1818 Yorkshire, England	1848
Rupert Brooke	1887 Warwickshire, England	1915
Gary Brooker	*not available*	
Elizabeth Barrett Browning	1806 Durham, England	1861
Robert Browning	1812 London, England	1889
Roy Campbell	1902 Durban, South Africa	1957
Charles Causley	1917 Cornwall, England	
Samuel Taylor Coleridge	1776 Somerset, England	1849
Dick Davis	1945 Portsmouth, England	
Emily Dickinson	1830 Massachusetts, USA	1886
Patric Dickinson	1914 Nasirabad, India	
Mbella Sonne Dipoko	1936 Cameroun	
John Donne	1572 London, England	1631
Thomas Stearns Eliot	1888 St Louis, USA	1965
Robert Frost	1874 San Francisco, USA	1963
Thomas Gray	1716 London, England	1771
John Gurney	1935 Bedfordshire, England	
Thomas Hardy	1840 Dorset, England	1928
Seamus Heaney	1939 County Derry, Ireland	
Philip Hobsbaum	1932 London, England	
John Holloway	1920 London, England	
Gerard Manley Hopkins	1844 Essex, England	1889
Ted Hughes	1930 Yorkshire, England	
Elizabeth Jennings	1926 Lincolnshire, England	
Ben Jonson	1572 Westminster, England	1637
John Keats	1795 London, England	1821
Philip Larkin	1922 Coventry, England	
David Herbert Lawrence	1885 Nottinghamshire, England	1930
Cecil Day Lewis	1904 Sligo, Ireland	1972
Edward Lucie-Smith	1933 Kingston, Jamaica	
Louis MacNeice	1907 Belfast, Ireland	1963
Andrew Marvell	1621 Yorkshire, England	1678
Roger McGough	1937 Liverpool, England	
John Milton	1608 London, England	1674

Mervyn Morris	1937 Kingston, Jamaica	
Edwin Muir	1887 Orkney, Scotland	1959
Sir Henry Newbolt	1862 Staffordshire, England	1938
Norman Nicholson	1914 Cumberland, England	
Abioseh Nicol	Sierra Leone	
Gabriel Okara	1921 Nigeria	
Wilfred Owen	1893 Shropshire, England	1918
Coventry Patmore	1823 Essex, England	1896
Brian Patten	1946 Liverpool, England	
Lenrie Peters	1932 Bathurst, The Gambia	
Sylvia Plath	1932 Boston, USA	1963
Cole Porter	1891 Indiana, USA	1964
Frank Templeton Prince	1912 Kimberley, South Africa	
Rodney Pybus	1938 Newcastle-upon-Tyne, England	
Keith Reid	1946, London, England	
Christina Rossetti	1830 London, England	1894
Dante Gabriel Rossetti	1828 London, England	1882
Michael Schmidt	1947 Mexico City	
William Shakespeare	1564 Stratford-upon-Avon, England	1616
Percy Bysshe Shelley	1792 Sussex, England	1822
Wole Soyinka	1934 Abeokuta, Nigeria	
Skip Spence	1946–1999, Ontario, Canada	
Stephen Spender	1909 London, England	
James Stephens	1882 Dublin, Ireland	1950
Alfred, Lord Tennyson	1809 Lincolnshire, England	1892
Dylan Thomas	1914 Swansea, Wales	1953
Edward Thomas	1878 London, England	1917
Ella Wheeler Wilcox	1850 Wisconsin, USA	1919
William Wordsworth	1770 Cumberland, England	1850
Thomas Wyatt	1503 Kent, England	1542
William Butler Yeats	1865 Dublin, Ireland	1939